ETHEL MERMAN

Ethel Merman as Annie Oakley in Irving Berlin's *Annie Get Your Gun*, by Rosemarie Sloat, 1971. National Portrait Gallery, Smithsonian Institution, Washington, D.C./Art Resource, N.Y.

ETHEL MERMAN

A Bio-Bibliography

George B. Bryan

Bio-Bibliographies in the Performing Arts, Number 27

GREENWOOD PRESS
New York • Westport, Connecticut • London

Library of Congress Cataloging-in-Publication Data

Bryan, George B.
    Ethel Merman : a bio-bibliography / George B. Bryan.
      p. cm.—(Bio-bibliographies in the performing arts, ISSN
  0892-5550 ; no. 27)
    Discography: p.
    Includes bibliographical references and index.
    ISBN 0-313-27975-6 (alk. paper)
    1. Merman, Ethel—Bibliography. 2. Merman, Ethel—Discography.
  I. Title. II. Series.
  ML134.5.M47B8 1992
  782.1'4'092—dc20
  [B]   92-6428

British Library Cataloguing in Publication Data is available.

Library of Congress Catalog Card Number: 92-6428
ISBN: 0-313-27975-6
ISSN: 0892-5550

First published in 1992

Greenwood Press, 88 Post Road West, Westport, CT 06881
An imprint of Greenwood Publishing Group, Inc.

Printed in the United States of America

The paper used in this book complies with the
Permanent Paper Standard issued by the National
Information Standards Organization (Z39.48-1984).

10 9 8 7 6 5 4 3 2 1

With respect and admiration, this book is dedicated to

RICHARD MOODY,

teacher, scholar, and friend.

"Better than a thousand days of diligent study is one day with a great teacher."

Contents

Preface

As a graduate student, I encountered Jane Ellen Harrison's influential *Prolegomena to the Study of Greek Religion*, all 682 pages of it. Think of it: nearly 700 pages of *introduction* to a subject! Little did I think that in a distant day I would publish 300 pages of introduction to the life and career of another kind of phenomenon, Ethel Merman. True, Merman wrote two autobiographies and has been the subject, so far, of one biography and one doctoral dissertation. While each has its merits, none offers the breadth of documentation contained in this bio-bibliography.

Few reference books, I suspect, are completed without the assistance of numerous people. In particular, I wish to acknowledge

Orlin R. and Irene Corey, who encouraged my initial interest in Merman and added substantially to my collection of Merman artifacts;

Kelly C. Morgan, who rendered valuable research assistance in New York, and Veronica C. Richel, my colleague at the University of Vermont, who expertly read and commented on the manuscript;

Leith Adams of the Warner Brothers Archives at the University of Southern California; Ross C. Allen, professor emeritus of Indiana University; Richard Buck of the New York Library of the Performing Arts at Lincoln Center; Ned Comstock of the Cinema-TV Library at the University of Southern California; Andrea Comtois, my associate in the Department of Theatre at the University of Vermont; Catherine De Meis of Andrew Solt Productions; Susan King of Merv Griffin Enterprises; and Susan Morse of the Bailey-Howe Library at the University of Vermont, all of whom supplied otherwise inaccessible and pertinent information;

Robert Gardiner, Merman's concert agent, who was my link with Merman herself as well as my introduction to Steve Cole and Roger Hayes, whose archives and personal recollections of Merman enrich this work immeasurably.

THE FORMAT OF THIS BOOK

This reference book presents the facts and some observations about Merman's life and career in an easily accessible format. The first section consists of a narrative biographical essay that refers to but does not detail her many theatrical activities.

A chronology of the major episodes of the Merman story precedes sections devoted to her work in films, the stage, radio and television, and recordings. The largest component of the book, however, is the annotated bibliography, which represents the most extensive list of materials on Merman yet published. An index completes the volume.

Biography

Prodigal indeed is the twentieth century, reputed to allow everyone fifteen minutes of fame, for upon Ethel Merman it bestowed fifty-five years of unmitigated celebrity. In a career encompassing cabaret, vaudeville, recordings, radio, television, films, and the concert stage, Merman dominated the American musical stage as no other performer has, yet she appeared in only fifteen Broadway productions between 1930 and 1970.

Hers is not the story of an adolescent escape from loveless poverty to the theatre nor one of a ceaseless struggle for professional preeminence. Quite the contrary. She enjoyed a comfortable, middle-class existence with sympathetic parents who survived and shared her life into the mid-1970s. Her first Broadway role brought renown; her fourth, the appellation "queen of musical comedy." After that, Merman assumed almost mythical proportions.

The Merman name on the marquee above the title was a virtual guarantee of a successful run. Every new appearance was greeted with vigorous enthusiasm, and even after she announced her retirement from the Broadway stage, first in 1961, then again in 1970, there was always hope that she would change her mind and work the Merman magic one more time.

On stage Merman revealed herself unequivocally, but the offstage Merman continues to be elusive. Separating the real Merman from the persona she fabricated out of the roles she played on and off the stage is a hazardous undertaking. At her best, in life as in the theatre, she was disciplined, demanding, forthright, and irreverent; she was also sentimental, romantic, generous, and, most of all, vulnerable.

What follows, then, is the story of an entertainer whose chronological development may conveniently be divided, like Gaul, into three parts: (1) Merman the prodigious, 1912-39, (2) Merman the peerless, 1940-70, and (3) Merman the phenomenal, 1971-84. For the sake of discussion, her offstage life and her professional activities in each period are presented separately, although they were, of course, interdependent.

Merman the Prodigious (1912-39)

Ascending from comfortable circumstances at home to the brink of stardom in the theatre constituted the first phase of Merman's prodigious career. The life of Ethel Agnes Zimmermann, her baptismal name, was comfortable, unremarkable, and uncomplicated. Her father, Edward Zimmermann, had a good job as a bookkeeper at a wholesale dry goods company, and her mother, Agnes Zimmermann (née Gardner), worked in the home at 359 Fourth Avenue, Astoria, Queens, NY.

Merman contended that she was born on 16 January 1912, but there is considerable con-

fusion as to the actual date. Since she would
have been only eighteen at the opening of *Girl
Crazy* in 1930 and therefore in conflict with
the child labor laws, she claims to have added
the necessary three years to appear an adult
twenty-one. The resulting 1909 birthdate appears in nearly all the reference sources
since there was no reason to doubt the au-
thenticity of this "official" statistic. Merman's biographer, however, cites the year as
1908 without documentation or explanation.[1]

Her childhood years, though not entirely
halcyon, inculcated a sense of security, family, and self-reliance, virtues that sustained Merman in her professional life. She
attended Public School #4 and then opted for
a four-year secretarial course at William
Cullen Bryant High School. Although her en-
suing work as a secretary at the Bragg-
Kliesrath Corporation was pleasant and satisfying, her boss' theatrical contacts fed her
already strong desire to be an entertainer.

Merman's advancement in the theatre, in
films, and on recordings was meteoric. She
never received vocal training, but from an
early age her powerful voice pleased and surprised her family and friends. The young Merman sang often as an amateur, her reception
increasing her self-confidence. Merman served
a brief theatrical apprenticeship in cabaret
and vaudeville and profitably used this time
to add technique to her natural gifts. Continuing to work as a secretary while gaining

---

[1]Bob Thomas, *I Got Rhythm: The Ethel Merman Story*
(New York: G. P. Putnam's Sons, 1985): 16. Although
official records can easily clarify this issue, the New
York Bureau of Vital Records will provide a birth
certificate only to members of the immediate family,
but not to curious scholars. Mister Thomas did not
respond to an invitation to document the 1908
birthdate.

valuable performance experience, Merman registered with several agents and sang wherever she could.

While appearing in September 1929 at a nightclub called Little Russia, Merman was heard and signed by agent Lou Irwin, who arranged for her to join the Clayton, Jackson, and Durante show at their cabaret, Les Ambassadeurs. Merman enjoyed working with the good-hearted Jimmy Durante and was well-received by the patrons, but a tonsillectomy forced her withdrawal from the show.

After she recuperated and filled some club dates in Miami, Merman returned to New York and, at Irwin's suggestion, put together an act with pianist/arranger Al Siegel. The team had a promising start at their first appearance at the Ritz Theatre in Elizabeth, NJ. Encouraged by journalists and audiences alike at several subsequent bookings,[2] they proved extremely viable at the Brooklyn Paramount Theatre. After attracting considerable attention at the Pavilion Royale in Valley Stream, Long Island, Merman and Siegel scaled the pinnacle of achievement in vaudeville, playing the Palace Theatre in Manhattan. This legendary mecca of the variety stage proved to be her springboard onto the musical comedy stage.

Merman performed in seven Broadway productions in this period, and each represented a personal triumph for her. Vinton Freedley, producer of George Gershwin's forthcoming show, *Girl Crazy* (1930), saw Merman at the Brooklyn Paramount and asked her to meet the

---

[2] At an engagement in White Plains, Merman and Siegel performed before Lela McMath Rogers and her daughter, actress Ginger. Some time later, Lela Rogers suggested to Vinton Freedley that Merman be auditioned for the role of "Kate Fothergill." Ginger Rogers, *Ginger: My Story* (New York: HarperCollins, 1991): 69, 74.

composer at his elegant apartment. Gershwin, playing three songs from the score of *Girl Crazy*, said, "Miss Merman, if there's anything about these songs you don't like, I'll be most happy to change it." Overcome by Gershwin's gesture, Merman stammered, "No, Mr. Gershwin, they'll do very nicely." As a result of this interview, Merman was cast in the role of "Kate Fothergill."

The writers Howard Lindsay and Russel Crouse, impressed at rehearsals by Merman's native talent for comedy, continually enlarged her part. The raw beginner who went into re-hearsals emerged on opening night as a show-stopper. When Merman, clad in a red blouse and a black satin slit skirt, launched into the mildly suggestive number, "Sam and Delilah," the audience received her wildly. Soon after-wards, holding onto a high C in "I Got Rhythm" for sixteen bars, Merman unleashed pandemonium that demanded numerous encores. Gershwin, im-pressed by Merman's performance, went to her dressing room at intermission and advised her never to go near a singing teacher. Stopping the show in her first Broadway appearance, Merman was on the way to stardom, a conclusion about which the reviewers left no doubt.

The eleventh edition of *George White's Scandals* was in difficulty in its out-of-town tryout, so Merman was added to strengthen the cast. While vacationing with her parents in Lake George, NY, she had been summoned by White to see the floundering revue in Atlantic City. Merman joined Rudy Vallee, Alice Faye, Willie and Eugene Howard, Everett Marshall, Ray Bolger, and others in the cast in Newark, NJ, on 1 September 1931. After two weeks' "shakedown" rehearsal, the *Scandals* opened in New York. Merman sang "Life Is Just a Bowl of Cherries" (among other numbers) and once again gathered critical plaudits.

Her next show, *Humpty Dumpty*, despite a formidable collaborative team, closed out of town but was refashioned as *Take a Chance* (1932) and enjoyed a respectable run. Merman had the enviable opportunity to shine in a bawdy ballad called "Eadie Was a Lady," the story of a hooker who had class with a capital "K." Luxuriating in the success of the production, Merman took to the road and performed in Chicago for only two weeks before withdrawing because of throat problems.

Cole Porter's *Anything Goes* (1934) became a milestone in Merman's career. Analyzing her voice and delivery, Porter provided her in the role of "Reno Sweeney" tailor-made, showstopping songs such as "Anything Goes," "You're the Top," "Blow, Gabriel, Blow," and "I Get a Kick out of You." *Anything Goes* brought Merman her longest run (420 performances) to date as well as superlative reviews.

Merman and Porter had proven to be a winning team, but, despite the best of intentions, *Red, Hot, and Blue!* (1936) did not surpass their previous effort. Porter, again fashioning his words and music to his star's style, contributed "Ridin' High" and the torchy "Down in the Depths on the 90th Floor." Hampered by a weak book, Merman, Jimmy Durante, and Bob Hope nevertheless achieved considerable personal comedic success. "Merman reigns supreme as the exponent of a style she seems to have invented (**B258**)," a critic noted.

No one was surprised by the mediocre reception of *Stars in Your Eyes* (1939), which was insubstantial from the beginning. Costarring again with Jimmy Durante, Merman played a movie star, "Jeanette Adair," in love with a leftist film director. "This Is It" and "I'll Pay the Check" were her best songs, but Arthur Schwartz and Dorothy Fields, the composer and lyricist, while gifted, were not of the caliber of George and Ira Gershwin and Cole Porter. *Stars in Your Eyes*, jinxed by the Depression and in competition with the New York World's Fair, could not survive for more than a respectable 127 performances.

Porter indicated his interest in doing another show with Merman, so *Du Barry Was a Lady* (1939) happily co-starred her with Bert Lahr. The critics either delighted in or decried the patent vulgarity of the show, but *Du Barry Was a Lady* with Merman as club singer "May Daly" and Lahr as washroom attendant "Louis Blore" attracted large, appreciative audiences. In addition to "Friendship," the showstopper duet that Merman sang with Lahr, she also excelled in the plaintive "Do I Love You?" Producer B. G. De Sylva, realizing that the actress' powers were then fully developed, determined that Merman was ready for solo stardom.

Merman entered films early in her career, but despite favorable critical reactions, she found the medium unsatisfying. While she was still singing in nightclubs in 1929, Merman signed a contract with Warner Brothers (Vitaphone) to make musical shorts. After waiting months for a script, she was cast in *The Cave Club*, which was filled with inanities. Then, when no further cinematic work presented itself, she was determined to extract herself at any cost from her obligation to Warners'.

Despite this inauspicious introduction to films, in 1930 Merman appeared with Ed Wynn and Ginger Rogers in Paramount's *Follow the Leader*. Since she came across well in this picture, Paramount offered Merman a contract to film short musical subjects, which proved to be pleasant work.

Merman then appeared with Bing Crosby and
Carole Lombard in *We're not Dressing* (1934),
the first of a string of depressing experi-
ences for the singer, who despised Hollywood's
methods of work and cliquish social mores. Her
big number with a chorus line of dancing elephants, "It's the Animal in Me," excised from
We're not Dressing, was interpolated into *The
Big Broadcast of 1936* (1935). Being paid for
appearing in two pictures but actually working
on one proved a satisfactory recompense for
her disappointment.

Merman contracted to act in *Kid Millions*
(1934) when Samuel Goldwyn offered the opportunity to co-star with Eddie Cantor. The high
point of this film is a haunting if somewhat
over-produced version of "First You Have Me
High, Then You Have Me Low." Since the Cantor-
Merman chemistry proved popular, they were
reunited in *Strike Me Pink* (1936), a better
than usual Cantor vehicle because of Merman's
presence (**B80**). Her rendition of "An Earful of
Music" is quintessential 1930s.

When in 1936 *Anything Goes* was adapted
for filming, Merman reprised her role of "Reno
Sweeney." The next motion picture in which she
appeared, *Happy Landing* (1938), starred Sonja
Henie and Don Ameche and featured the stars
and Merman on ice skates. Some of Merman's
best cinematic work, which she did in *Alexander's Ragtime Band* (1938), was left on the
cutting room floor. She then played in
Straight, Place, and Show (1938), a farrago of
Ritz Brothers nonsense, before she distanced
herself from films for a long time.

Merman first entered the recording studio
to make the soundtracks of her films, but it
was the discs of her stage numbers that established her as a singer of popular music. In
1932 Merman recorded "How Deep Is the Ocean?"
and "I'll Follow You" from *George White's*

Scandals. Her strongest songs from *Take a Chance* and *Anything Goes*, "Eadie Was A Lady," "I Get a Kick out of You," and "You're the Top," were released by Brunswick Records in the mid-'30s.

Radio beckoned the young Merman, principally for guest appearances with performers like Gus Van and Jimmy Durante. In 1935 Merman conducted a well-received twelve-week, thirty-minute musical variety show called *Rhythm at 8*, which continued without her when she left New York to honor film commitments in Hollywood.

Remembering her initial successes in cabaret and variety, Merman entered into a thirty-week engagement at the Casino in the Park soon after *Girl Crazy* opened (1930). Only months later (June 1931), she did her solo act at the New York Paramount, where Rudy Vallee was the headliner, and then at the Palace Theatre with Lou Holtz as emcee. In 1932 she sang again at the Palace on the bill with Jack Haley. Before starting rehearsals for *Anything Goes* (1934), Merman was back at the Paramount with George Jessel. Perhaps foreshadowing the final phase of her career was her contribution to the Gershwin Memorial Concert on 9 August 1937 in which she sang with a symphony orchestra in the Lewisohn Stadium to over 24,000 people.

Merman the Peerless (1940-70)

Progressing to the pinnacle of success both as a singer and an actress while pursuing elusive personal happiness were the hallmarks of the second segment of Merman's development. She appreciated the strength of her parents' marriage, but circumstances dictated the ultimate failure of her four marital alliances.

William Smith,[3] her first husband, was an agent who worked in California while Merman pursued her career in New York. Recalling this marriage, Merman wrote, ". . . there was no way the marriage could work. I realize now I hardly knew the man. I got into it too soon. It was a mistake. But we all make mistakes. That's why they put erasers on pencils (**B307**, p. 117)." Her second husband, Robert Daniels Levitt, a journalist and publisher, was, perhaps, her one great love and the father of her children. With reference to the collapse of this union, Merman said, "Bob was traveling a lot. . . and we stood by helplessly while our marriage slowly deteriorated. Neither of us had any idea of what to do (**B307**, p. 167)." Robert F. Six, the third husband, was an airline executive who prompted Merman's temporary retirement from the theatre to live in Denver, CO. Six's alleged philandering and unorthodox use of her money were Merman's reasons for this divorce. Actor Ernest Borgnine remained her husband for only thirty-eight days. So angered by his treatment of her, Merman entitled a blank page of her last autobiography "My Marriage to Ernest Borgnine."

As the mother of two children, she delighted in their upbringing despite its impingement upon her career. Ethel Merman Levitt was born on 20 July 1941, while her father was still serving in the U. S. Army. Enjoying her maternal role, but like all parents, not un-

---

[3]In her last autobiography (**B307**), Merman calls him William R. Smith on p. 11 and William B. Smith on p. 116. Is this a typographical error or confusion, since the man's middle name appears to be Jacob? Bob Thomas (**B537**, p. 77) says Bill Smith died in 1984, but the obituary in *Variety* (12 Oct. 1983) records that William Jacob Smith died at the Motion Picture Home in Woodland Hills, CA, on 8 Oct. 1983. The former agent is quoted as asking, "How much 'I Got Rhythm' can a man take before breakfast?"

failingly successful, Merman reshaped her
habits insofar as possible to accommodate
Ethel's changing needs. Reluctant at first to
sanction Ethel's marriage in 1960, Merman
eventually gave her blessing and delighted in
becoming a grandmother. Although even she
recognized signs of growing mental instability
in her daughter, Merman was devastated by the
news of Ethel's death on 23 August 1967 from
an overdose of medication.[4]

On 11 August 1945 Robert Daniels Levitt,
Jr., who was the last of Merman's children,
made his appearance. In Bobby's company both
as a child and an adolescent, Merman made several trips to Europe and Asia and later encouraged his career as a theatrical lighting
designer. Bobby's reluctance to "settle down,"
concerned his mother, but she nevertheless de-
pended upon him for support. Constantly at-
tending Merman during her last illness, Bobby
eased her final days.

Merman was a lifelong Republican, but her
political involvements crossed party lines.
Despite her inherited political convictions,
Merman sang the national anthem for one of
Franklin D. Roosevelt's presidential campaigns
and performed at his birthday parties. She
supported the Eisenhower presidential candidacy at a fundraiser at Madison Square Garden
in February 1952, her allegiance being reward-
ed by invitations to sing at the Republican
National Convention both in 1952 and 1956. Although her Republican loyalties were a matter
of record, she entertained at one of the Ken-
nedy inaugural parties on 20 January 1961.
Predictably, she would actively campaign for

---

[4]Merman always maintained that it was prescribed
medication that killed Ethel, but the newspaper ac-
counts reported that it was a simple overdose, implying
the misuse of controlled substances.

and occasionally socialize with Richard Nixon and Ronald Reagan.

Merman, the epitome of the gum-chewing, wisecracking, tough-as-nails New Yorker, engaged in numerous charitable works. When the U. S. entered World War II, Merman regularly entertained the troops at Camp Shanks. She assisted the American Theatre Wing, which staged a fundraiser for the British War Relief Society, and sang in *It's Fun to Be Free*, staged by Billy Rose at the Golden Horseshoe in 1943. When Mayor Robert Wagner inaugurated New York's Summer Festival in 1957, Merman served as the official hostess. She added to her extensive art collection by purchasing a painting by a stripper in the cast of *Gypsy* at a charity auction.

Merman's career in all phases of the entertainment industry reached dizzying heights, but it was in musical comedy that she honed and practiced her matchless gifts before displaying them in other venues. Receiving solo star billing for the first time, Merman scored a hit in *Panama Hattie* (1940). She described her character, "Hattie Maloney," as "quite a dame. Hattie was a brassy broad who hung out with sailors and didn't speak correct, but she had a softer side (**B307**, p. 112)." Hattie's big numbers were "Make It Another Old-Fashioned, Please" and "Let's Be Buddies," sung with winsome child actress, Joan Carroll.

Called "the missing link between Lily Pons and Mae West (**B335**)," Merman had another winner in Cole Porter's *Something for the Boys* (1943). Rosamond Gilder concluded that in the part of "Blossom Hart," Merman acted "with a minimum of gesture and a maximum of innuendo (**B181**)." In September 1944 Merman went into a show called *Sadie Thompson* but withdrew from it after twelve days' rehearsal.

Annie Get Your Gun (1946), with 1,147 performances, was Merman's longest lasting production and the first Broadway musical to exceed 1,000 performances. Irving Berlin provided songs that would ever afterwards be associated with Merman: "Doin' What Comes Natur'lly," "You Can't Get a Man with a Gun," "They Say It's Wonderful," "Moonshine Lullaby," "I'm an Indian Too," "I Got Lost in His Arms," "I Got the Sun in the Morning," "Anything You Can Do, I Can Do Better," and the irrepressible "There's No Business Like Show Business." Of Berlin, she wrote, "With all due respect to the Gershwins and Cole, Irving had given me range, allowing me a kind of vulnerability that was missing in girls like 'Nails' Duquesne, Blossom Hart and Hattie Maloney (**B307**, p. 139)."

Berlin's *Call Me Madam* (1950) provided Merman one of her best roles, that of "Sally Adams," U. S. Ambassador to Lichtenburg, clearly inspired by the life of famous party-giver and ambassadress Perle Mesta. The librettists, Howard Lindsay and Russel Crouse, constantly made changes in the script even after the show was supposed to be "frozen," which occasioned one of Merman's most quoted "zingers." Prior to the New York opening, Merman announced, "Boys, as of right now I am Miss Birdseye of 1950. I am frozen. Not a comma (**B307**, p. 164)." The musical hit of the show was a counterpoint number, "You're Just in Love."

Happy Hunting (1956), a reflection of the Grace Kelly-Rainier of Monaco nuptials, was Merman's next vehicle. According to her, it was "a jeep among limousines. You had to tend to business, shifting gears and feeding the gas to keep it moving when the going got rough, but if you didn't mind the bumpy ride, it got you there (**B307**, pp. 197-198)." The only song from *Happy Hunting* that achieved currency apart from the stage is "Mutual Admiration Society," but the slightly risqué "Mr. Livingstone" is a delight.

Given the meatiest role of her career, that of the frustrated, overbearing stage mother of Gypsy Rose Lee, Merman reached new heights in *Gypsy* (1959), adding a sensitive characterization to her much lauded vocal and comedic accomplishments. "I don't say this just because I created her," writes Merman, "but Mamma Rose is the most memorable character ever portrayed in any musical, with all due respect to Nellie Forbush, Liza Doolittle, or any of the rest (**B307**, p. 203)." "Some People" and "Everything's Coming up Roses" were eminently worthwhile additions to Merman's repertoire, but in "Rose's Turn" she created "an electrifying piece of bravura (**B209**)" that is assured a permanent place in the theatre's annals.

Merman, twenty years after her initial triumph as sharpshooter "Annie Oakley," appeared in a revival of *Annie Get Your Gun* (1966). In addition to her original songs, Berlin gave Merman a new counterpoint tour de force, "Old Fashioned Wedding." A reviewer noted that "as the song says, 'There's No Business Like Show Business,' and there's no show business like Ethel Merman's (**B293**)."

The role of matchmaking "Dolly Gallagher Levi" in *Hello, Dolly!* (1970), created by Carol Channing, was conceived with Merman in mind and became her final vehicle in musical comedy. Two songs that add significant depth to Dolly's character were restored to the score when Merman joined the cast: "World, Take Me Back" and "Love, Look in My Window." With Merman as the seventh actress in the eponymous role, *Hello, Dolly!* became Broadway's longest-running production at that time.

It was on the cabaret stage, however, that Merman rediscovered the audience that had received her indulgently in her apprentice-ship. Appearing in Las Vegas for the first time, she played to capacity houses, enjoyed the intimate contact with audiences, but found the noisy, smoky atmosphere uncongenial. Convinced, nevertheless, that club dates could be financially rewarding as well as creatively satisfying, the singer assembled *The Ethel Merman Show* and performed to great acclaim throughout the country. English and Australian audiences likewise received her enthusias-tically.

Although Merman's work in films in the 1930s had been disappointing to her, her later appearances were somewhat more fortuitous. More than seventy guest stars, including Mer-man, made brief appearances in *Stage Door Canteen* (1943). In a song called "Marching through Berlin," she "swell[ed] out into some-thing that is the best part of joy, getting full bounty from the worst lyric of the war **(B155)**." For *Call Me Madam* (1953) Merman re-ceived glowing critical notices, one of them calling her "a constant fascination in action and in song. . . **(B68)**." Merman's next film, *There's No Business Like Show Business* (1954), only marginally less critically successful than *Call Me Madam,* was her last starring role in motion pictures and one of her happiest ex-periences in film. Although she had some good moments in *It's a Mad, Mad, Mad, Mad World* (1963), Merman's performance was not an abso-lute comedic triumph. A critic conceded, how-ever, that she "may be flashy, noisy, and even naively vulgar, but her zest for life is un-quenchable **(B219)**." These qualities were also evident in *The Art of Love* (1965), in which she played a gaudy bordello keeper.

Radio appearances continued to enhance Merman's national reputation. She sang the theme song of a pre-war propaganda show called *Keep 'Em Rolling* (1941) and performed as a guest on Bing Crosby's show (1948). *The Ethel Merman Show* (1949) was an unsuccessful attempt to put her in a sustaining series.

Merman enjoyed an intermittent presence on television, but her success in this medium reflected rather than advanced her stage career. Appearing with Mary Martin on the *Ford 50th Anniversary Show* (1953), Merman sang to the largest TV audience to date. She recalled that "the director placed Mary in front of a poster from *South Pacific* and me in front of one from *Call Me Madam*. From there we walked over to two stools set against a plain background and he just let us sing. The simplicity of the concept had such impact that everybody copied us. Every television variety show that you watched after our appearance had the star and guest sitting on two barstools singing medleys, but we did it first (**B307**, p. 186)."

Merman, assisted by Frank Sinatra and Bert Lahr, reprised her "Reno Sweeney" in a bastardized version of *Anything Goes* (1954). In an abbreviated *Panama Hattie* (1954), Ray Middleton, Art Carney, and Jack E. Leonard were her associates.

Visited in her home in Denver, CO, by the cameras of Edward R. Murrow, Merman was the featured guest on *Person to Person* (1955). On the *General Electric Theatre* (1956) and the *U. S. Steel Hour* (1956), Merman extended her range to straight dramatic roles.

Although it was planned and produced by competent artists, *Ethel Merman on Broadway* (1959) failed to meet expectations. "We laid a giant dinosaur's egg," Merman recalled. "The point is that in show business it takes more than hard work, experience and talent. You can have the best intentions, a good idea, all the

know-how, *but* if you don't have luck nothing
else helps (**B307**, p. 208)." Then there were
stints on *The Gershwin Years* (1961), *The Bob
Hope Show* (1962), and two sensational segments
of *The Judy Garland Show* (1963, 1964). *Maggie
Brown* (1963) was an unsuccessful pilot for a
situation comedy starring Merman. She was then
(1964) a guest on Lucille Ball's program, appearing in a hilarious episode called "Lucy
Teaches Ethel Merman to Sing." In 1965 she
played a straight dramatic role on the *Kraft
Suspense Theatre*. A tabloid version of the
revived *Annie Get Your Gun* was televised in
1967, after which Merman played continuing
roles in Marlo Thomas' *That Girl* (1967) as
well as in *Batman* (1967) and *Tarzan* (1967).

Merman, under exclusive contract to Decca
Records, was no stranger in the recording stu-
dios and did some of her best work during this
period. Decca released four of Merman's numbers from *Panama Hattie* as well as the original cast album of *Annie Get Your Gun*. Taking
advantage of her growing reputation, Decca
then pressed *Ethel Merman: Songs She Has Made
Famous*. When RCA won the rights to issue the
original cast recording of *Call Me Madam*, Merman, supported by Dick Haymes, offered selections from the musical on the Decca label.

Combining previously recorded songs and
new ones, *Ethel Merman: The World Is Your Balloon* features several duets with Ray Bolger
and Jimmy Durante. The soundtrack album of
Call Me Madam teamed Merman with George Sanders and Donald O'Connor.

The recording of the *Ethel Merman and
Mary Martin Duet from the Ford 50th Anniver-
sary Show* was a runaway seller. *There's No
Business Like Show Business*, issued as another
soundtrack album, featured Merman, Dan Dailey,
Donald O'Connor, Mitzi Gaynor, and Johnnie
Ray. Decca appealed to both nostalgia and

novelty by recording Merman in *Memories: 40 Great Songs from the Gay '90s to the Roaring '20s*. The two-record album *Ethel Merman: A Musical Autobiography* contains representative songs from her long career as well as an irradiating first-person narrative. Disguising its mediocrity by her galvanism, Merman was featured on the original cast album of *Happy Hunting*. The original cast album of *Gypsy*, documenting Merman's most riveting performance in a musical and now available on compact disc, is of transcendent importance. *Merman. . . Her Greatest!*, recorded in the wake of her towering success in *Gypsy*, is a retrospection of the songs she made famous.

Merman in Vegas reveals the mature artist as well as the ambiance of her first engagement in the gambling capital, but the quality of the recording is poor. *Annie Get Your Gun* showcases Merman and the original cast of the revival. The singer herself produced *Ethel Merman Sings the New Songs from Hello, Dolly!*, the best extant record of her last role in the musical theatre.

Aside from the adulation of audiences, Merman received numerous tokens of distinction. She was, for example, on the cover of *Time* (1940) and was bidden to participate for the first of two times in the Royal Command Variety Performance (1955). Her work in *Happy Hunting* was recognized by a Tony nomination and the Barter Theatre Award and that in *Call Me Madam* by both the Tony (for the stage play) and the Hollywood Correspondents' Awards (for the film). *Gypsy* brought the New York Drama Critics' Circle Award for best actress in a musical and a nomination for the Tony. In 1966 she was voted Woman of the Year by the Hasty Pudding Club of Harvard University.

Merman the Phenomenal (1971-84)

Sustaining and enhancing her status as a theatrical phenomenon and maintaining her personal equilibrium were the work of Merman's declining years. She withstood with fortitude the loss of her parents and her own declining health while undertaking pleasurable professional ventures. Her mother, Agnes Gardner Zimmermann, died on 14 January 1974, and her father, Edward Zimmermann, on 22 December 1977.

Merman's strong constitution enabled her to pursue her many interests, but her health slowly, almost imperceptibly deteriorated. As signs of her grudging descent into old age and illness, Merman tripped in the finale of a TV special, experienced a troublesome blackout while taping another show, was hospitalized because of a painful sciatic nerve, and grew intermittently volatile in her behavior to both friends and foes. After collapsing in her apartment on 7 April 1983, she subsequently was discovered to have an inoperable brain tumor. Surrounded in her apartment by the mementos of an active life, Merman slowly, reluctantly surrendered all hope of recovery.

In the theatre Merman enjoyed the luxury of basking in her own legendary status. Although she excluded the possibility of acting in another musical, Merman forged a new, productive career as a solo performer. In *The Ethel Merman Show* format, she sang her standards accompanied either by a theatre orchestra or a pianist. She was a great success in a two-week engagement at London's beloved home of variety entertainment, the Palladium (1974). Then came a proposal to sing with Mary Martin in a tandem concert such as they had done on the *Ford 50th Anniversary Show*, so they collaborated to great acclaim on *Together on Broadway* (1977).

After a successful concert in 1975 with the Boston Pops Orchestra, Merman shared concert stages with symphony orchestras across the country. During this period, Merman, who had infrequently sung outside New York, reached audiences before which she had never played. In *The Ethel Merman in Concert* arrangement, the first part of the program typically was devoted to orchestral selections and the second to Merman. A reviewer of her performance at the Hollywood Bowl (1978) concluded that she had "the greatest singing voice in the nonoperatic musical theatre **(B315)**." The last of these concerts seems to have been with the Philadelphia Orchestra (1981), but their momentum culminated in what was virtually her farewell performance in New York, that at Carnegie Hall on 3 May 1982.

Films no longer tempted Merman, but she took pleasure in the briefest of cameo appearances in *Airplane!* (1980). "In one flashback scene, the fighter-pilot hero finds himself in a mental ward with other battle-scarred veterans. The fellow in the next bed, he explains to his sweetheart, is so deranged 'he thinks he's Ethel Merman.' Whereupon Ethel Merman rises from the bed and sings a few bars of 'Everything's Coming Up Roses' **(B537**, p. 203)."

Television frequently beckoned, and sometimes Merman responded, with varying degrees of success. Ralph Edwards genuinely surprised Merman by featuring her on *This Is Your Life* (1971).[5] She then performed with Jack Lemmon in *'S Wonderful, 'S Marvelous, 'S Gershwin* (1972) and in *Ed Sullivan's Broadway* (1973).

---

[5]This segment of *This Is Your Life* was repeated on 25 February 1984, soon after Merman's death.

Believing her 1975 concert with the Boston Pops Orchestra to be extraordinary, conductor Arthur Fiedler's producers saved the show to be telecast on 4 July 1976 as part of the national bicentennial celebration. In that same year TV audiences saw her on the *Ted Knight Musical Comedy Variety Special*.

Merman launched an ill-fated pilot for a situation comedy, *You're Gonna Love It Here*, in 1977. In a continuing role as Gopher's mother, Merman acted in four episodes of *The Love Boat* (1979, 1980, 1981, 1982). Sylvia Fine was her director in *Musical Comedy Tonight* (1979) on PBS. After singing on the *Texaco Star Theater: Opening Night*, she was reunited with her old friend, Mary Martin, on her PBS program for senior citizens, *Over Easy* (1982), the climax of which was a duet of "Anything I Can Do, You Can Do Better" [sic].

American recording companies were no longer interested in her, but principally under the aegis of their British counterparts, Merman still delivered some vocal surprises. Supported by lush orchestrations, she recreated her classics on *Merman Sings Merman*. The singer, Stanley Black, and the London Festival Orchestra joined forces again to record *Annie Get Your Gun*. On *Ethel's Ridin' High*, she sang a couple of her old songs and interpreted quite a number of standards. A & M Records then released *The Ethel Merman Disco Album*, consisting of her standards with an overlaid disco beat.

Honor heaped upon distinction characterized the final phase of Merman's life. The Actors' Fund recognized her charitable works in 1970. In 1972 she received a special Tony award for her career accomplishments, which was followed by her election to the Theater Hall of Fame. The National Academy of Popular Music bestowed the Johnny Mercer Award on Merman in 1980, and in 1982 she received ASCAP's Pied Piper Award. In that same year her rendition of "There's No Business Like Show Business" comprised the finale of the Royal Command Variety Performance, the theme of which was timeless musicals.

Death came to Ethel Merman on 15 February 1984. Now that she cannot surprise us once again with a memorable performance, what can be said of her remarkable fifty-five-year career? What sustained her so long in a profession noted for its short memory and in the estimation of audiences given to fickleness? At the beginning and at the end, there was a voice, a voice so indescribable that writers exhausted the thesaurus in the attempt:

> ". . . one sighs with satisfaction at the perfection of her [vocal] technique. . . ."

> ". . . for her to pretend to any modesty about her vocal gifts would be wanton affectation."

> ". . . the voice is . . . thrilling and always unforgettable."

> "She has the finest enunciation of any American singer I know. She has a sense of rhythm which few can equal."

> ". . . a train announcer's contralto."

"Broadway's only female tenor"

". . . not a human voice. It's another instrument in the band."

". . . an instrument of untrammelled resonance."

"a doll from Astoria with a trumpet in her throat"

"the hard forthrightness of a jazz trumpet--an ability to stay on pitch while she shouts at the top of her lungs."

". . . the trumpet-tonsiled Merman voice is always in the winner's circle."

"a voice with the hard, clarion forthrightness of a jazz trumpet"

"a raucous overtone to the trumpets of a band. . . a soft trill for a torch song. . . tinny for a parody. . . ."

"The Midas touch is upon her tonsils because she can turn brass into gold. She can do more than that. She can keep it brass."

"Hell, it's quite an organ. It's got ping. I

guess she's got leather down there."

"a voice like a calliope"

"Her throat houses as beguiling a calliope as Broadway knows."

"singing like a boat whistle"

"a razzle-dazzle voice, a perfect sense of time, and impeccable diction"

". . .the ultimate in big league vocalizing."

In addition to the voice, there was Merman's natural comedic gift. Again critics searched for ways to describe her performances:

". . .every line she reads. . . is as illuminated as the most dazzling of Times Square's electric signs."

"laughed uproariously at Merman's down-to-earth deportment"

"the best of the comics. . . Ethel Merman and Martha Raye on the distaff side."

". . . she just naturally drips comedy the way some trees drip maple syrup."

"the comedy touch of an
old pro"

"such a firm grasp of the
art of comic acting that
she practically has it by
the throat."

"Her comic sense is every
bit as authoritative, as
high-handed really, as
her singing voice."

"a comedienne of rare
skill, who combines rich-
ness and warmth with her
humor"

"She knows comedy as
thoroughly as she knows
singing. . . ."

Finally, there was her presence, that
unmistakable quality that distinguishes a star
from a mere technician:

"monumental, magnificent,
and miraculous"

". . . a vitality that
dominates. . . like a
cyclone."

"To refer to our planet
as plundered when Miss
Merman can be counted
among its inexhaustible
resources is to make a
travesty of science. . .
."

"one of the theatre's
titans"

"the heartbeat of show business"

". . . her personal magnetism electrifies the whole theatre. . . . a performer of incomparable power."

"the apparent ease and skill with which she can take such unquestionable command of a huge audience."

"like watching a train hurtle down the tracks, undeviating, the whole performance radiating zest and spontaneity"

"the exponent of a style she seems to have invented. . . . a combination of superficial blatancy with subtle undercurrents of nuance and satire. . . ."

"Like other miracles, Ethel Merman has to be seen and heard to be believed."

"There is no more potent musicomedy fuel on Broadway than Ethel Merman."

"the undisputed number one musical comedy songstress"

". . . the Everest of American musical comedy

simply because she's
there. . . . the pres-
ence has all the subtlety
of a block of marble. . .
."

"the energy of a bulldoz-
er"

"the urgency of a steam
calliope, the assurance
of an empress, and a lik-
able low-downness all her
own."

"They say greatness is an
elusive quality, some-
thing impossible to de-
scribe. It wasn't . . .
when Ethel sang. You
could see it, and feel
it."

". . . the strength and
poise of the Empire
State. . . and a rare
ability to charge rou-
tines with excitement."

"the strutting incarna-
tion of style in American
musicals"

". . . an itch that
couldn't be scratched, a
brushfire claiming a
whole mountainside, a pop
and a snap and a crackle.
. . like a freshly tapped
gusher with the sound
soaring high in the air,
straight up and off into
eternity."

". . . her vitality is so
exceptional, and her in-
stinct for emotional ex-
pression so impulsive. .
. ."

"Nobody since Alexander
the Great has had quite
the confidence of Mer-
man."

"the most commanding min-
strel in the business"

"in her finest form, of
which there is nothing
finer"

". . .the illustrious
American institution. . .
one of the joys of the
world"

"everything that her spe-
cial raucous ebullient
genius should be"

"The reasons for her ap-
peal are unfathomable. It
is the perpetual riddle
of genius."

Those who never saw Merman on the stage
and must rely on recordings, motion pictures,
and dim memories of televised performances may
perhaps find it difficult to reconcile their
impressions with the foregoing reactions. Like
Merman, Laurence Olivier electrified the stage
to a degree only hinted at even in his finest
filmed performances. The living theatre was
the Olympus on which Merman and Olivier
reigned as titans. Their artistic conceptions,
admittedly on different planes, transcended

the real world and achieved an almost al-
chemic, but highly theatrical immediacy in the
actual presence of audiences.

Merman's larger-than-life characterizations, her idiosyncratic voice, and her pre-
sentational style sometimes overpowered the
motion picture and television screens that
tend to value fidelity to real life above all
else; the recorded voice, divorced from the
characterizations of which it was part, sometimes created an aural surfeit. In the cavern-
ous theatres that traditionally housed her
Romantic musical comedies, however, Merman's
unabashed, grandiose theatricality seemed not
only appropriate but also necessary.

Had she been more a technical and less an
instinctive performer and therefore more
adaptable, Merman might have conquered the me-
chanical media as completely as she did the
stage. Had she aspired to be a popular vocal-
ist rather than a singing actress, she might
have shaped her style of singing according to
current trends. Had she been less identified
with the Gershwins, Porter, Berlin, Styne, and
Sondheim, she might have reached audiences
that ignored her as passé. Had she not been
such a quintessential New Yorker and eschewed
extensive touring, she might have had wider
geographical appeal. Such speculation is, of
course, idle. Merman did exactly what she
wanted to do; she could not have remained
Merman and done less.

Chronology

16 Jan. 1912	Ethel Agnes Zimmermann is born at 359 4th Avenue, Astoria, NY. (The dates 16 Jan. 1908 and 1909 have also been given. See **B537**.)
1917	Merman sings at local military bases.
Sept. 1929	Merman is booked to sing for two weeks at the Little Russia night club for $60 per week.
	Merman signs film contract with Warner Brothers and makes a jungle short called *The Cave Club*.
Oct. 1929	Merman performs with Clayton, Jackson and Durante at Les Ambassadeurs for $85 per week.
	While recuperating from a tonsillectomy, Merman sings at the Roman Pools

Casino in Miami Beach, FL for $300 per week.

Merman casts her lot with pianist/arranger Al Siegel and breaks in their act at the Ritz Theatre in Elizabeth, NJ.

Merman and Siegel perform at the Brooklyn Paramount, where she is seen by producer Vinton Freedley, and on weekend nights at the Pavilion Royal in Valley Spring on Long Island.

10 Sept. 1930	*Her Future*, the first of Merman's eight short films for Paramount, is released.
13 Sept. 1930	Merman and Siegel play two-a-day vaudeville at the Palace Theatre, NY.
12 Oct. 1930	Merman appears in film *Follow the Leader*.
14 Oct. 1930	*Girl Crazy* opens at the Alvin Theatre, NY., for which Merman earns $375 per week.
1930	Merman sings songs from *Girl Crazy* on Louis Calhern's radio show.
4 Nov. 1930	Merman opens a 30-week engagement at the Casino in the Park, NY, for which she is paid $1,250 per week.

4	Jan.	1931	Merman speaks but does not sing on Gus Van's radio show.
27	Feb.	1931	Merman's short film *Devil Sea* is released.
	Mar.	1931	Merman returns to the Casino in the Park.
	June	1931	*Girl Crazy* closes. Merman appears at the Paramount Theatre, NY, where Rudy Vallee is the headliner.
	July	1931	Merman performs at the Palace Theatre, NY, where Lou Holtz is the emcee.
14	Sept.	1931	*George White's Scandals* opens at the Apollo Theatre, NY. Merman earns $1,250 per week.
	Oct.	1931	Merman records three songs from the *Scandals*.
27	Nov.	1931	Merman's short film *Roaming* is released.
	Jan.	1932	Merman sings at the Casino in the Park, NY.
18	Mar.	1932	Merman's short film *Old Man Blues* is released.
	Apr.	1932	*George White's Scandals* closes.
24	Apr.	1932	Merman opens at the Palace Theatre, NY, with Jack Haley.

19	May	1932	Merman's short film *Let Me Call You Sweetheart* is released.
30	June	1932	Merman's short film *Ireno* is released.
1	Aug.	1932	Merman's short film *You Try Somebody Else* is released.
	Sept.	1932	Merman contracts to make sixteen recordings for the RCA-Victor company.
26	Sept.	1932	*Humpty Dumpty* opens at the Nixon Theatre, Pittsburgh, PA.
28	Sept.	1932	Merman records for RCA-Victor.
26	Nov.	1932	*Take a Chance* opens at the Apollo Theatre, NY.
15	Dec.	1932	Merman sings "I Surrender, Dear" on radio.
16	Dec.	1932	Merman records "Eadie Was a Lady."
22	Dec.	1932	Merman's short film *Time on My Hands* is released.
17	Jan.	1933	Merman's short film *Song Shopping* is released.
16	Feb.	1933	Merman's short film *Be Like Me* is released.
		1933	Merman performs in *Take a Chance* in Chicago, IL, for two weeks.

	Sept.	1933	Merman sings at the Paramount Theatre, New York.
	Sept.	1933	Merman and her mother visit Hollywood for the first time.
26	Apr.	1934	Merman's film *We're not Dressing* is released.
27	Apr.	1934	Merman and George Jessel head the bill at the New York Paramount Theatre.
8	Oct.	1934	Merman records "An Earful of Music."
17	Oct.	1934	Merman appears in the film *Kid Millions*.
21	Nov.	1934	*Anything Goes* opens at the Alvin Theatre, NY.
4	Dec.	1934	Merman records "I Get a Kick out of You" and "You're the Top."
	Feb.	1935	Merman's recordings of "You're the Top" and "I Get a Kick out of You" are #1 in New York.
5	May	1935	Merman performs for twelve weeks in a successful radio series, *Rhythm at 8*.
13	July	1935	Merman leaves the cast of *Anything Goes* to honor her movie contract.
17	July	1935	Merman records "The Lady in Red" and "It's the Animal in Me."

		"It's the Animal in Me" is inserted into the film *The Big Broadcast of 1936*.
14	Jan. 1936	Merman appears in the film *Strike Me Pink*.
5	Feb. 1936	Merman films *Anything Goes*.
11	Apr. 1936	Merman's act is seen at the Paramount Theatre, New York.
7	Aug. 1936	Merman and her parents sail for Europe on the *Normandie*.
29	Oct. 1936	*Red, Hot, and Blue!* opens at the Alvin Theatre, NY.
6	Nov. 1936	Merman records "Down in the Depths," "It's De-Lovely," "Ridin' High," and "Red, Hot, and Blue."
	Apr. 1937	Merman performs in *Red, Hot, and Blue!* in Chicago, IL, for two weeks.
13	July 1937	Merman contributes to a memorial to George Gershwin on radio.
9	Aug. 1937	Merman sings in the Gershwin Memorial Concert in Lewisohn Stadium, NYC.
22	Jan. 1938	Merman appears in the film *Happy Landing*.

28	May	1938	Merman appears in the film *Alexander's Ragtime Band*.
	Sept.	1938	Merman opens at the Strand Theatre, NY.
20	Sept.	1938	Merman sings "Marching Along with Time" on radio.
28	Sept.	1938	Merman appears in the film *Straight, Place, and Show*.
		1939	Merman sings "It's All Yours" on radio with Jimmy Durante.
9	Feb.	1939	*Stars in Your Eyes* opens at the Majestic Theatre, NY.
22	Feb.	1939	Merman records "A Lady Needs a Change," "I'll Pay the Check," "This Is It," and "Just a Little Bit More."
6	Dec.	1939	*Du Barry Was a Lady* opens at the 46th Street Theatre, NY.
28	Oct.	1940	Merman's picture is on the cover of *Time*.
30	Oct.	1940	*Panama Hattie* opens at the 46th Street Theatre, NY.
15	Nov.	1940	Merman marries William Jacob Smith at Elkton, MD.

	1941	Merman is divorced by William J. Smith.
	1941	Merman marries Robert D. Levitt in Connecticut.
20 July	1941	Ethel Merman Levitt is born.
9 Nov.	1941	Merman sings the theme song of *Keep 'Em Rolling* on the Sun Mutual radio network.
7 Jan.	1943	*Something for the Boys* opens at the Alvin Theatre, NY.
12 May	1943	Merman appears in film *Stage Door Canteen*.
Apr.	1944	Merman has a miscarriage.
18 Sept.	1944	Merman begins rehearsing *Sadie Thompson*.
30 Sept.	1944	Merman withdraws from *Sadie Thompson*.
12 Jan.	1945	Merman and William Gaxton perform on radio's *Stage-door Canteen*.
11 Aug.	1945	Robert Daniels Levitt, Jr., is born.
16 May	1946	*Annie Get Your Gun* opens at the Imperial Theatre, NY.
11 June	1947	Merman is a guest on Bing Crosby's radio show.

19	Feb.	1948	*Annie Get Your Gun* closes.
22	Mar.	1948	Merman makes an appearance on Milton Berle's TV show.
20	June	1949	Merman stars in an episode of a CBS-TV program called *Thru the Crystal Ball*.
20	June	1949	Merman sings with tenor Lauritz Melchior on *The Ford Show*.
31	July	1949	*The Ethel Merman Show* proves to be an unpromising radio experiment.
12	Oct.	1950	*Call Me Madam* opens at the Imperial Theatre, NY, with Merman earning $6,000 per week.
5	Nov.	1950	Merman participates in the inaugural broadcast of radio's *The Big Show*, on which she will often appear.
8	Feb.	1952	Merman sings "There's No Business Like Show Business" at a fundraiser called *They Like Ike* at Madison Square Garden
	Apr.	1952	*Call Me Madam* closes.
5	May	1952	Merman opens the road tour of *Call Me Madam* in Washington, DC.

7	June	1952	Merman is divorced from Robert D. Levitt in Juarez, Mex.
	July	1952	Merman sings at the Republican National Convention in San Francisco, CA.
9	Mar.	1953	Merman marries Robert F. Six in Mexicali, Mex.
12	Mar.	1953	Merman's film *Call Me Madam* is released.
29	Mar.	1953	Ed Sullivan welcomes Merman to his TV show for the first of numerous times.
15	June	1953	Merman and Mary Martin star in TV's *Ford 50th Anniversary Show.*
	Oct.	1953	*The Ethel Merman Show* is featured at the Texas State Fair.
24	Jan.	1954	Merman welcomes Jimmy Durante to TV's *Colgate Comedy Hour.*
28	Feb.	1954	Merman's *Anything Goes* is televised.
10	Nov.	1954	*Panama Hattie*, with Merman in her old role, is shown on television.
8	Dec.	1954	Merman appears in the film *There's No Business Like Show Business.*

25 Jan. 1955   Merman sings on TV's *Shower of Stars.*

14 Apr. 1955   *Ethel Merman's Show Stoppers* is televised on the *Shower of Stars.*

17 July 1955   Ed Sullivan welcomes Merman to his TV show, *Toast of the Town.*

9 Sept. 1955   Merman is featured on Edward R. Murrow's *Person to Person.*

7 Nov. 1955   Merman appears at Royal Command Variety performance at the Palladium Theatre, London.

6 Dec. 1955   Merman is a guest on TV's *The Chevy Show* with Bob Cummings.

25 Mar. 1956   Merman appears on *The General Electric Theater* (TV).

9 May 1956   Merman acts on TV in *Honest in the Rain.*

Aug. 1956   Merman sings at the Republican National Convention in San Francisco, CA.

6 Dec. 1956   *Happy Hunting* opens at the Majestic Theatre, NY.

May 1957   Merman receives the Barter Theatre Award.

30 Nov. 1957   *Happy Hunting* closes.

27 Jan. 1958	Merman's former husband, Robert D. Levitt, commits suicide.
21 May 1959	*Gypsy* opens at the Broadway Theatre, NY.
1959	Merman receives the New York Drama Critics' Circle award for best actress in a musical.
1959	Merman is nominated to receive the Tony award for her performance in *Gypsy*.
24 Nov. 1959	*Merman on Broadway* is televised.
Dec. 1960	Merman is divorced from Robert F. Six.
15 Jan. 1961	Merman sings on TV in *The Gershwin Years*.
20 Jan. 1961	Merman entertains at John F. Kennedy's inaugural celebration.
29 Mar. 1961	In *Gypsy* Merman starts her most extensive road tour in Rochester, NY.
Apr. 1962	Merman sings a medley of Berlin tunes on the *Academy Awards Show*.
25 Oct. 1962	Merman opens at the Flamingo, Las Vegas, NV, for $40,000 per week.
20 Nov. 1962	Merman is a guest on Bob Hope's TV show.

	1963	*The Ethel Merman Show* plays summer dates in tents and outdoor theatres.
22 Sept.	1963	Merman sings in the show celebrating the opening of Lincoln Center (NY).
23 Sept.	1963	*Maggie Brown*, an unsuccessful TV pilot, features Merman in the leading role.
6 Oct.	1963	Merman makes her first appearance on the *Judy Garland Show* (TV).
7 Nov.	1963	Merman appears in film *It's a Mad, Mad, Mad, Mad World*.
12 Jan.	1964	Merman is seen again on the *Judy Garland Show* (TV).
28 Jan.	1964	Merman joins the tribute to Cole Porter on TV's *Bell Telephone Hour*.
Feb.	1964	Merman appears at London's Talk of the Town.
13 Apr.	1964	Merman sings at the 36th Academy Awards ceremony.
1 June	1964	Merman is a guest on *The Lucy Show* (TV).
	1964	Merman appears on British TV's *Val Parnell's Sunday Night at the Palladium*.

26 June 1964	Merman marries Ernest Borgnine.
6 May 1965	Merman appears in film *The Art of Love.*
3 June 1965	Merman acts in *'Twixt the Cup and Lip* on TV's *Kraft Suspense Theatre.*
7 July 1965	Merman is divorced from Ernest Borgnine.
1965	Merman appears at the Sheraton Hotel in Sydney, Australia.
Mar. 1966	Merman is named Woman of the Year by Harvard's Hasty Pudding Club.
31 May 1966	*Annie Get Your Gun* opens at the New York State Theatre.
28 Sept. 1966	*Annie Get Your Gun* opens at the Broadway Theatre, NY.
19 Mar. 1967	Television audiences see Merman in an abbreviated *Annie Get Your Gun.*
23 Aug. 1967	Ethel Merman Levitt dies.
7 Sept. 1967	Marlo Thomas features Merman as a guest on *That Girl* (TV).
5 Oct. 1967	Merman makes her first appearance on TV's *Batman.*

1	Dec.	1967	Merman plays a singing missionary on TV's *Tarzan*.
1	Feb.	1968	Merman reappears on *That Girl* (TV).
5	May	1968	Merman celebrates Irving Berlin's birthday on a special *Ed Sullivan Show* (TV).
	July	1968	Merman performs *Call Me Madam* with the St. Louis Municipal Opera.
8	Sept.	1968	Merman appears on *Around the World of Mike Todd* (TV).
		1969	Merman's *Call Me Madam* is seen in Kansas City, MO.
20	Apr.	1969	Merman is a presenter on *The Tony Awards Show* (TV).
28	Mar.	1970	Merman joins the cast of *Hello, Dolly!*.
	Oct.	1970	The Actors' Fund of America commends Merman for outstanding service and generosity.
20	May	1971	Ralph Edwards honors Merman on *This Is Your Life* (TV).
17	Jan.	1972	Merman appears with Jack Lemmon in *'S Wonderful, 'S Marvelous, 'S Gershwin* (TV).

23	Apr.	1972	Merman receives a special Antoinette Perry (Tony) Award.
	Oct.	1972	The Theater Hall of Fame and Museum inducts Merman.
16	Mar.	1973	Merman is featured on *Ed Sullivan's Broadway* (TV).
14	Jan.	1974	Agnes Gardner Zimmermann, Merman's mother, dies.
9	Sept.	1974	Merman opens a two-week engagement at the Palladium Theatre, London
2	May	1975	Merman participates in the salute to Joshua Logan in aid of the City Museum of New York.
4	July	1976	Merman's concert with Arthur Fiedler and the Boston Pops Orchestra is aired on TV.
16	Sept.	1976	Merman appears with the Nashville (TN) Symphony Orchestra.
27	Sept.	1976	Merman helps to inaugurate TV's *The Big Event*.
26	Oct.	1976	Merman nominates Gershwin, Porter, and Berlin to the Entertainment Hall of Fame (TV).
30	Nov.	1976	*The Ted Knight Musical Comedy Variety Special* (TV) features Merman.

10	Mar.	1977	Merman participates in the first of two *Merv Griffin Shows* dedicated to "the belters."
16	Mar.	1977	Merman appears with the Wichita (KS) Symphony Orchestra.
15	May	1977	Merman and Mary Martin are reunited in *Together on Broadway*.
1	June	1977	Merman stars in the pilot telecast of *You're Gonna Love It Here*.
6	June	1977	Merman appears with the Seattle (WA) Symphony Orchestra.
10	June	1977	Merman appears with the Dallas (TX) Symphony Orchestra.
14	July	1977	Merman appears with the Chatauqua (NY) Symphony Orchestra.
22	July	1977	Merman appears with the Denver (CO) Symphony Orchestra.
	Aug.	1977	Merman appears in concert at the Hollywood Bowl.
22	Dec.	1977	Edward Zimmermann, Merman's father dies.
29	Jan.	1978	Merman appears with the Indianapolis (IN) Symphony Orchestra.

3   Feb.   1978   Merman appears with the
                       Detroit (MI) Symphony
                       Orchestra.

11 Feb.   1978   Merman appears with the
                       Kansas City (MO) Philhar-
                       monic Orchestra.

18 Apr.   1978   Merman appears with the
                       Norfolk (VA) Symphony Or-
                       chestra.

27 July   1978   Merman appears with the
                       Philadelphia (PA) Orches-
                       tra.

11 Aug.   1978   Merman appears with the
                       Los Angeles (CA) Philhar-
                       monic at the Hollywood
                       Bowl.

16 Sept. 1978   Merman appears with the
                       Minnesota Orchestra.

24 Nov.   1978   Merman appears with the
                       Hamilton (Ont.) Philhar-
                       monic.

3   Dec.   1978   *Christmas Eve on Sesame
                       Street* features Merman.

10 Jan.   1979   Merman performs on TV's
                       *American Pop: The Great
                       Singers.*

13 Mar.   1979   Merman appears with the
                       North Carolina Symphony
                       Orchestra.

30 Mar.   1979   Merman appears with the
                       Springfield (MA) Symphony
                       Orchestra.

12 May 1979	Merman makes her first appearance as Gopher's mother on TV's *The Love Boat*.
9 June 1979	Merman appears with the Milwaukee (WI) Symphony Orchestra.
20 June 1979	Merman appears with the Atlanta (GA) Symphony Orchestra.
8 July 1979	Merman appears with the Baltimore (MD) Symphony Orchestra.
20 July 1979	Merman appears with the South Dakota Symphony Orchestra.
12 Sept. 1979	Merman appears with the Syracuse (NY) Symphony Orchestra.
1 Oct. 1979	Merman sings three songs from *Anything Goes* on *Musical Comedy Tonight*.
4 Nov. 1979	Merman appears with the Springfield (MA) Symphony.
25 Nov. 1979	Merman's voice is heard in *Rudolph & Frosty's Christmas in July* (TV).
17 Mar. 1980	Merman receives the Johnny Mercer Award of the National Academy of Popular Music.

3	May	1980	Merman appears with the Richmond (VA) Symphony Orchestra.
27	Oct.	1980	Merman sings "There's No Business Like Show Business" on Beverly Sills' retirement telecast.
11	Nov.	1980	Merman is briefly seen in the film *Airplane!*.
19	Jan.	1981	Merman sings at the Ronald Reagan Inaugural Celebration.
27	Apr.	1981	Merman joins George Burns on TV's *100 Years of America's Popular Music*.
9	May	1981	Merman appears with the Roanoke (VA) Symphony Orchestra.
18	June	1981	Merman appears with the Philadelphia Orchestra.
	Feb.	1982	Merman receives ASCAP's Pied Piper Award.
8	Mar.	1982	Merman is seen on TV's *Night of 100 Stars*.
3	May	1982	Merman appears in concert at Carnegie Hall, NY.
25	May	1982	Merv Griffin celebrates Merman's Carnegie Hall concert and her receipt of the Pied Piper Award on his TV show.
11	Sept.	1982	*The Texaco Star Theater: Opening Night* is tele-

vised with Merman in the cast.

8 Nov. 1982   Merman sings in the Royal Command Variety Performance.

Apr. 1983   Merman undergoes surgery to remove a brain tumor.

15 Feb. 1984   Merman dies in her apartment in Manhattan.

20 Feb. 1984   The lights of Broadway are dimmed in Merman's honor.

25 Feb. 1984   The Merman installment of *This Is Your Life* is retelecast.

1 Mar. 1984   The entertainment industry pays tribute to Merman at the Huntington Hartford Theatre in Hollywood, CA.

4 May 1985   Merman is seen on *Broadway: A Special Salute* (TV), which was filmed earlier.

Filmography

F01   *THE CAVE CLUB*
          (Vitaphone; 15 May 1930; 9 minutes)

Cast

Marjorie Leach	Frank Tinney
Frank Pierlot	**Ethel Merman**
Harriet Harbaugh	Ted Lewis

Synopsis

This short film is "a subject with song and dance, in two scenes--one a primitive Night Club with Amazon gals doing their stuff --then a mystic glass and one gets an insight into night life of today, giving the idea that entertainment tastes have changed but little (**B338**)."

Commentary

About this film, Merman remembers, "For some reason, now better forgotten, I was running around in a bear skin. Very chic. Finally Indians chased me up a tree, whereupon I burst into song. It was the craziest thing I've ever been associated with (**B307**, p. 33)."

Review: See **B338**.

F02   *FOLLOW THE LEADER*
               (Paramount; 12 December 1930; 76
               minutes)

Credits

Based on *Manhattan Mary* by William K. Wells,
George White, B. G. De Sylva, Lew Brown, and
Ray Henderson

Director   Norman Taurog
Screenplay   Gertrude Purcell,
                                Sid Silvers
Dialogue Director   Al Parker

Cast

Crickets   Ed Wynn
Mary Brennan   Ginger Rogers
Helen King   **Ethel Merman**

Stanley Smith, Lou Holtz, Lida Kane, Bobby
Watson, Donald Kirke, William Halligan, Holly
Hall, Preston Foster, James C. Morton

Synopsis

A brassy understudy gets her big break
when the leading lady is kidnapped.

Commentary

Of this and the next seven short features, Merman says, "Primitively developed
stories received little help from slapdash
production. But I got the idea that making
movies could be fun (**B307**, p. 61)."

F03   *HER FUTURE*
               (Paramount; 10 September 1930)

Credits

Director/Screenplay   Mort Blumenstock

Commentary

Merman sings "My Future Just Passed" and "Sing, You Sinners."

F04   *DEVIL SEA*
            (Paramount; 27 February 1931)

Credits

Director/Screenplay   Mort Blumenstock
Musical arranger   Al Siegel

F05   *ROAMING*
            (Paramount; 27 November 1931)

Credits

Director/Screenplay   Casey Robinson
Songs   Johnny Green

Synopsis

Merman, "the daughter and shill of a traveling medicine man," sings "Hello, My Lover, Goodbye" and "Shake Well Before Using."

F06   *OLD MAN BLUES*
            (Paramount; 18 March 1932)

Credits

Director   Aubrey Scotto
Story   J. P. Murray,
                                Barry Travers,
                                Ben Oakland

F07   *LET ME CALL YOU SWEETHEART*
            (Paramount; 19 May 1932; 8 minutes)

Credits

Director   Dave Fleischer

Animators	James H. Culhane, David Tendlar
Composers/ lyricists	Beth Slater Whitson, Leo Friedman

Commentary

This is a singalong film in which Merman sings the song, first published in 1910, then leads the audience while the lyrics are flashed upon the screen. The animation consists of a bouncing ball above the lyrics.

Review: See **B499**.

F08   *IRENO*
(Paramount; 30 June 1932; 9 minutes)

Credits

Director	Aubrey Scotto
Screenplay	Aubrey Scotto, Andrew Bennison

Synopsis

"Reno is the scene and Ethel is about to divorce hubby. She is losing her dough at the roulette table at the same time. In a blue mood she sits down in a corner, sees shadows upon the wall, bursts into a ballad while the shadows, changing, tell the story of her busted romance. Hubby reappears and after saying 'never' twice, Ethel says 'yes' and they clinch (**B498**)."

Commentary

"Wipe That Frown Right off Your Face" is Merman's number in this film.

Review: See **B498**.

F09   *YOU TRY SOMEBODY ELSE*
            (Paramount; 1 August 1932)

Credits

Director   Dave Fleischer
Composers/Lyricists   B. G. De Sylva, Lew
                        Brown, Ray Henderson

Commentary

In this singalong film Merman introduces a current (1931) hit song and then invites the audience to sing it with her.

F10   *BE LIKE ME*
            (Paramount; 16 February 1933)

Credits

Director/Screenplay   Casey Robinson

Commentary

Merman sings "After You've Gone."

F11   *TIME ON MY HANDS*
            Paramount; 22 December 1932; 10
            minutes)

Credits

Director   Dave Fleischer
Animators   Willard Bowsky,
                               Thomas Goodson
Lyrics   Harold Adamson, Mack Gordon
Music   Vincent Youmans

Review: See **B500**.

F12   *SONG SHOPPING*
            (Paramount; released 18 May 1933; 7
            minutes)

Credits

Director	Dave Fleischer
Animators	Willard Bowsky,
	David Tendlar

Review: See **B510**.

F13   *WE'RE NOT DRESSING*
(Paramount; 26 April 1934; 77 minutes)

Credits

Director	Norman Taurog
Producer/Story	Benjamin Glazer
Screenplay	Horace Jackson,
	Francis Martin,
	George Marion, Jr.
Music	Harry Revel,
	Mack Gordon

Cast

Stephen Jones	Bing Crosby
Doris Washington	Carole Lombard
George	George Burns
Gracie	Gracie Allen
Edith	**Ethel Merman**
Hubert	Leon Errol
Prince A. Stofani	Jay Henry
Prince M. Stofani	Raymond Milland
Old Sailor	John Irwin
Captain	Charles Morris
1st Ship's Officer	Bill Hendricks
2nd Ship's Officer	Ted Oliver

Synopsis

Crosby, a shipwrecked sailor, becomes the easygoing ruler of a Pacific island, the inhabitants of which include Lombard, a spoiled heiress. He, of course, shows her the errors of her ways, and they fall in love.

Commentary

Merman's only song is "It's Just a New Spanish Custom," which she sings with Leon Errol and a chorus.

Reviews: See **B15**, **B69**, **B214**.

F14   *KID MILLIONS*
          (United Artists; 8 December 1934; 90 minutes; Video: Nelson Entertainment)

Credits

Director	Roy Del Ruth
Story/Screenplay	Arthur Sheekman, Nat Perrin, Nunnally Johnson
Editor	Stuart Heisler
Musical Director	Alfred Newman

Cast

Eddie	Eddie Cantor
Janet Larrabee	Ann Sothern
Dot	**Ethel Merman**
Jerry Lane	George Murphy
Ben Ali	Jesse Block
Fanya	Eve Sully
Col. Larrabee	Burton Churchill
Louie the Lug	Warren Hymer
Sheik Mulhulla	Paul Harvey
Khoot	Otto Hoffman
Toots	Doris Davenport
Herman	Ed Kennedy
Oscar	Stanley Fields
Adolph	John Kelly
Pop	Jack Kennedy
Stymie	Stymie Beard
Tommy	Tommy Bond
Leonard	Leonard Kilbrick
Slade	Guy Usher

Synopsis

The story, in Merman's words, is about "three flimflam artists trying to con little orphan Eddie out of his million-dollar inheritance. My part in the desperate scheme was to convince Eddie that I was his long-lost mother (**B307**, p. 65)."

Commentary

"An Earful of Music" is Merman's musical offering.

Reviews: See **B98**, **B336**.

F15   *THE BIG BROADCAST OF 1936*
             (Paramount; 26 September 1935; 94
             minutes)

Credits

Director	Norman Taurog
Producer	Benjamin Glazer
Screenplay	Walter De Leon,
Francis Martin, Ralph Spence	
Continuity	Jack Mintz
Editor	Ellsworth Hoagland
Songs	Ralph Rainger,
Richard Whiting, Leo Robin, et al.	

Cast

Bing Crosby	Wendy Barrie
Amos 'n' Andy	Benny Baker
Ethel Merman	Ina Ray Hutton
Guy Standing	Vienna Boys' Choir
David Holt	Lyda Roberti
Gail Patrick	Ray Noble
Bill Robinson	Jack Oakie
Mary Boland	Nicholas Brothers
C. Henry Gordon	Charlie Ruggles
George Burns	Gracie Allen

Synopsis

A very loose story about Jack Oakie's attempt to keep a radio station afloat strings together a variorum of variety acts seen through a proto-television receiver, the "radio eye."

Commentary

Merman's "It's the Animal in Me," filmed for *We're not Dressing* (**F13**) was spliced into this motion picture with the salutary effect of Merman's being paid twice for one job.

Reviews: See **B78**, **B113**.

F16   *STRIKE ME PINK*
            (United Artists; 22 January 1936;
            104 minutes)

Credits

Based on "Dreamland," a story by Clarence B.
     Kelland
Director   Norman Taurog
Adaptation/Screenplay   Frank Butler,
                             Walter De Leon,
                             Francis Martin
Additional Dialogue   Philip Rapp
Editor   Sherman Todd
Musical Director   Alfred Newman
Songs   Harold Arlen,
                                 Lew Brown

Cast

Eddie Pink   Eddie Cantor
Joyce   **Ethel Merman**
Claribel   Sally Eilers
Parkyakarkus   Harry Parke
Copple   William Frawley
Ma Carson   Helen Lowell
Butch   Gordon Jones

Vance	Brian Donlevy
Thrust	Jack La Rue
Sunnie	Sunnie O'Dea
Rita	Rita Rio
Killer	Edward Brophy
Chorley	Sidney H. Fields
Marsh	Don Brodie
Selby	Charles McAvoy
Miller	Stanley Blystone
Smiley	Duke York
Hardin	Charles Wilson
Pitchman	Clyde Hagar

and *the Goldwyn Girls*

Synopsis

In the words of Merman's biographer, the film is "patterned to. . . Eddie Cantor, who played a timid tailor with a secret love for a night club singer, Merman. The plot involved an amusement park and gangsters, combining chases with musical numbers. . . (**B527**, p. 57)."

Commentary

Merman's songs are "Shake It off with Rhythm," "Calabash Pipe," and "First You Have Me High, Then You Have Me Low."

Reviews: See **B80**, **B292**, **B340**, **B352**, **B368**.

F17   *ANYTHING GOES* [alternate title: *TOPS IS THE LIMIT*]
(Paramount; 30 January 1936; 92 minutes)

Credits

Director	Lewis Milestone
Producer	Benjamin Glazer
Songs	Cole Porter
Additional Songs	Leo Robins, Richard A. Whiting,

	Frederick Holland,
	Hoagy Carmichael,
	Edward Hayman
Editor	Eda Warren

Cast

Billy Crocker	Bing Crosby
Reno Sweeney	**Ethel Merman**
Rev. Dr. Moon	Charles Ruggles
Hope Harcourt	Ida Lupino
Bonnie La Tour	Grace Bradley
Sir Evelyn Oakleigh	Arthur Treacher
Elisha J. Whitney	Robert McWade
Bishop Dobson	Richard Carle
Mrs. Wentworth	Margaret Dumont
Detective	Edward Gargan
Ship's Captain	Matt Moore
Bearded Man	Rolfe Sedan

Commentary

Only three of Porter's songs are used: "Anything Goes," "You're the Top," and "I Get a Kick out of You." Merman also sings "Shanghai-de-Ho."

Reviews: See **B79**, **B341**.

F18   *HAPPY LANDING* [original title: *BREAD, BUTTER and RHYTHM*] (20th Century-Fox; 28 January 1938; 102 minutes)

Credits

Director	R. N. Bradbury
Producer	Paul Malvern
Story	Stuart Anthony
Screenplay	Gordon Rigby
Dialogue	Frances Hyland

Cast

Truly Ericksen	Sonja Henie
Jimmy Hall	Don Ameche
Herr Ericksen	Jean Hersholt
Flo Kelly	**Ethel Merman**
Duke Sargent	Cesar Romero
Counter Man	Billy Gilbert
Al Mahoney	Wally Vernon
Yonnie	El Brendel
Gypsy	Marcelle Corday
Agent	Joseph Crehan
Waiter	Eddie Conrad
Rink Manager	Ben Welden

and the *Raymond Scott Quintet*, *Peters Sisters*, and *Condos Brothers*

Synopsis

An airplane makes a forced landing in Norway, where the passengers meet Sonja Henie and her family. Naturally Ameche and Henie's characters fall in love.

Review: See **B81**.

F19   *ALEXANDER'S RAGTIME BAND* (20th Century-Fox; 11 August 1938; 106 minutes)

Credits

Director	Henry King
Screenplay	Kathryn Scola, Lamar Trotti
Adaptation	Richard Sherman
Musical Director	Alfred Newman

Cast

Alexander (Roger Grant)	Tyrone Power
Stella Kirby	Alice Faye
Charlie Dwyer	Don Ameche

Jerry Allen	**Ethel Merman**
Davey Lane	Jack Haley
Prof. Heinrich	Jean Hersholt
Aunt Sophie	Helen Westley
Taxi Driver	John Carradine
Bill	Paul Hurst
Wally Vernon	Himself
Ruby	Ruth Terry
Snapper	Douglas Fowley
Louie	Chick Chandler
Cpl. Collins	Eddie Collins
Stage Manager	Joseph Crehan
Eddie	Robert Gleckler
Specialty	Dixie Dunbar
Charles Dillingham	Joe King
Head Waiter	Charles Coleman
Colonel	Stanley Andrews

Synopsis

The vicissitudes of a troupe of performers from 1911 to 1938 are chronicled. Faye is marked for stardom in musical comedy, and Power and Ameche vie for her affection.

Commentary

Merman sings "Alexander's Ragtime Band," "Heat Wave," "Blue Skies," "A Pretty Girl Is Like a Melody," "Everybody Step," "Pack up Your Sins," and "Let's Go Slumming."

Reviews: See **B82**, **B114**, **B152**, **B219**.

F20   *STRAIGHT, PLACE, AND SHOW*
(20th Century-Fox; 30 September 1938; 66 minutes)

Credits

Based on a play by Damon Runyon and Irving
     Caesar
Director   David Butler

Screenplay	M. M. Musselman, Allen Rivkin
Additional Dialogue	Lew Brown
Songs	Lew Brown, Lew Pollack
Musical Director	Louis Silvers

Cast

Ritz Brothers	Themselves
Denny	Richard Arlen
Linda	**Ethel Merman**
Barbara Drake	Phyllis Brooks
Drake	George Barbier
Braddock	Sidney Blackmer
Truck Driver	Will Stanton
Russians	Ivan Lebedeff, Gregory Gaye, Rafael Storm
Slippery Sol	Stanley Fields
Terrible Turk	Tiny Roebuck
Promoter	Ben Welden
Detective	Ed Gargan
Referee	Pat McKee

Synopsis

Three operators of a children's pony ride find themselves the unlikely owners of a race horse. Posing a Russian jockeys, they mount up and enter an important race.

Review: See **B83**.

F21   *STAGE DOOR CANTEEN*
(United Artists; 14 June 1943; 135 minutes; Video: VCII, Inc.)

Credits

Director	Frank Borzage
Producer	Sol Lesser
Screenplay	Delmer Daves
Music	Freddie Rich

Musical Director   C. Bakaleinikoff
Editor   Hal Kern

Cast

Eileen   Cheryl Walker
"Dakota" Ed Smith   William W. Terry
Jean   Marjorie Riordan
"California"   Lon McAllister
Ellen Sue   Margaret Early
"Texas"   Michael Harrison
Mamie   Dorothea Kent
"Jersey"   Fred Brady
Lillian   Marion Shockley
The Australian   Patrick O'Moore
The Captain   Louis Jean Heydt
          and more than 70 guest stars,
          including **Ethel Merman**

Synopsis

The very thin plot concerns the rela-
tionships of four servicemen and the young
women they meet at the Stage Door Canteen,
where they are treated to performances by the
theatre's best.

Commentary

Merman sings "Marching through Berlin."

Reviews: See **B07, B84, B115, B155, B220, B434, B435.**

F22   *CALL ME MADAM*
          (20th Century-Fox; 5 March 1953;
          114 minutes)

Credits

Producer   Sol Siegel
Director   Walter Lang
Cinematographer   Leon Shamroy
Songs   Irving Berlin

Cast

Mrs. Sally Adams	**Ethel Merman**
Kenneth	Donald O'Connor
Princess Maria	Vera-Ellen
Cosmo Constantine	George Sanders
Pemberton Maxwell	Billy De Wolfe
Prince Hugo	Helmut Dantine
Tantinnin	Walter Slezak
Sebastian	Steven Geray
Grand Duke	Ludwig Stossel
Grand Duchess	Lilia Skala
Senator Brockway	Charles Dingle
Senator Gallagher	Emory Parnell
Senator Wilkins	Percy Helton
Bandleader	Leon Belasco
Chamberlain	Oscar Beregi
Miccoli	Nestor Paiva

Synopsis: See **S31**.

Commentary

Merman had left Hollywood years earlier as an unhappy supporting player, but she returned as a star for this film.

Reviews: See **B68**, **B246**, **B328**, **B560**.

F23   THERE'S NO BUSINESS LIKE SHOW BUSINESS
(20th Century-Fox; 17 December 1954; 117 minutes; Video: CBS/Fox Video)

Credits

Producer	Sol Siegel
Director	Walter Lang
Songs	Irving Berlin

Cast

Molly Donahue	**Ethel Merman**

Tim Donahue	Donald O'Connor
Vicky	Marilyn Monroe
Terrance Donahue	Dan Dailey
Steve	Johnnie Ray
Katy Donahue	Mitzi Gaynor
Lew Harris	Richard Eastham
Charles Gibbs	Hugh O'Brian
Eddie Dugan	Frank McHugh
Father Dineen	Rhys Williams
Marge	Lee Patrick
Helen	Eve Miller
Lillian Sawyer	Robin Raymon
Stage Manager	Lyle Talbot

Synopsis

Molly and Terry Donahue are successful vaudevillians who incorporate their three children into their act. Steve breaks up the family troupe by entering the priesthood, so the four Donahues continue to perform, each of the children forming romantic attachments along the way. Finally Tim and Katy get a chance to dance in a Broadway show, leaving Molly and Terry to continue alone. Tim, however, falls into dissipation and disappears. Terry goes off in search of Tim, and the whole family is reunited at a benefit performance while Molly sings "There's No Business Like Show Business."

Commentary

Response to this film was generally favorable, particularly to Merman's and Dailey's performances, but the predictable story, perhaps, kept it from being as popular as *Call Me Madam*.

Reviews: See **B22**, **B444**, **B561**.

F24   *IT'S A MAD, MAD, MAD, MAD WORLD*
(United Artists; 7 November 1963; 192 minutes; Video: CBS/Fox Video)

Credits

Producer, Director	Stanley Kramer
Story, Screenplay	William Rose,
	Tania Rose
Dir. Photog.	Ernest Laszlo
Addit'l. Photog.	Irmin Roberts,
	Hal McAlpin
Art Director	Gordon Gurnee
Set Decorator	Joseph Kish
Prod. Designer	Rudolph Sternad
Main Title	Saul Bass
Editors	Frederic Knudtson,
	Robert C. Jones,
	Gene Fowler, Jr.
Music	Ernest Gold
Make-up	George Lane,
	Lynn Reynolds
Costume Design	Bill Thomas

Cast

C. G. Culpeper	Spencer Tracy
J. Russell Finch	Milton Berle
Melville Crump	Sid Caesar
Benjy Benjamin	Buddy Hackett
Mrs. Marcus	**Ethel Merman**
Ding Bell	Mickey Rooney
Sylvester Marcus	Dick Shawn
Otto Meyer	Phil Silvers
J. A. Hawthorne	Terry-Thomas
Lennie Pike	Jonathan Winters
Monica Crump	Edie Adams
Emmeline Finch	Dorothy Provine
1st Cab Driver	Eddie Anderson
Tyler Fitzgerald	Jim Backus
Airplane Pilot	Ben Blue
Police Sergeant	Alan Carney
Mrs. Haliburton	Barrie Chase
Chief of Police	William Demarest
2nd Cab Driver	Peter Falk
Col. Wilberforce	Paul Ford
3rd Cab Driver	Leo Gorcey
Dinckler	Edward Everett Horton

Jimmy the Crook	Buster Keaton
Nervous Man	Don Knotts
Tower Control	Carl Reiner
Firemen	The 3 Stooges
Union Official	Joe E. Brown
Sheriff Mason	Andy Devine
Fire Chief	Sterling Holloway
Irwin	Marvin Kaplan
Airport Manager	Charles Lane
Airport Officer	Howard Da Silva
Lieutenant	Charles McGraw
Switchboard Operator	ZaSu Pitts
Police Secretary	Madlyn Rhue
Radio Tower Operator	Jess White
Mayor	Lloyd Bridges
Culpeper's Wife	Selma Diamond
Deputy Sheriff	Stan Freberg
Billie Sue	Louise Glenn
George	Ben Lessy
Pilot's Wife	Bobo Lewis
Miner	Mike Mazurki
Truck Driver	Nick Stuart
Chinese Laundryman	Sammee Tong
Detective	Stanley Clements
Detective	Norman Fell
Detective	Nicholas Georgiade
Smiler Grogan	Jimmy Durante
Police Officer	Allen Jenkins
Radio Operator	Harry Lauter
Salesman	Doodles Weaver
Traffic Cop	Tom Kennedy
Tower Radioman	Eddie Ryder
Helicopter Observer	Don Harvey
Patrolman	Roy Engle
Patrolman	Paul Birch
Man on Road	Jack Benny
Mad Driver	Jerry Lewis

Synopsis

When Smiler Grogan crashes his car and faces death, he admits that he has buried $350,000 of stolen money under the Big W at Santa Rosita Beach State Park. Four groups of larcenous treasure seekers embark by various means of transportation in search of the money. They are kept under surveillance by C. G. Culpeper, a captain of state police, who waits for them to lead him to the money, which he intends to steal for himself. Most of the film is devoted to the comic adventures of the four groups as their schemes to be the first to find the money go awry. Culpeper waits until they have discovered the fortune buried in a suitcase, but when he confiscates the bag and tries to make his escape, a great chase ensues. At the climactic moment, the suitcase comes open, the money is dispersed by the wind, and all the treasure seekers are losers. As Culpeper wonders if he will ever be able to laugh again, the loud, brazen Mrs. Marcus (Merman) slips on a banana peel.

Commentary

Merman recalls, "I was so overladen with costume jewelry that I clanked when I walked. And I used my white purse as a lethal weapon--almost. All in all, Mrs. Marcus was a wickedly funny shrew. . . (B307, p. 220)."

Reviews: See B221, B223, B247.

F25   *JOUNREY BACK TO OZ*
             (Filmation; 1964; 90 minutes; Video: United American, #5316)

Credits

Producers   Norm Prescott, Lou Scheimer
Director   Hal Sutherland

Cast

The voices of Liza Minnelli, Milton Berle, **Ethel Merman**, Margaret Hamilton, Mickey Rooney, and Paul Ford.

Synopsis

Dorothy and Toto revisit their friends in Oz and have to fight the wicked witch's sister.

F26   *THE ART OF LOVE*
             (Universal; 10 July 1965; 99 minutes)

Credits

Director	Norman Jewison
Producer	Ross Hunter
Screenplay	Carl Reiner
Story	Richard Alan Simmons, William Sackheim
Dir. Photography	Russell Metty
Art Director	Alexander Golitzen, George Webb
Set Decor	Howard Bristol, John P. Austin
Title	De Patie-Freleng
Editor	Milton Carruth
Music	Cy Coleman
Music Supv.	Joseph Gershenson
Choreographer	Hal Belfer
Costume Design	Ray Aghayan
Make-up	Bud Westmore

Cast

Casey Barnet	James Garner
Paul Sloan	Dick Van Dyke
Nikki Dunay	Elke Sommer
Laurie	Angie Dickinson
Mme. Coco La Fontaine	**Ethel Merman**
Rodin	Carl Reiner
Inspector Carnot	Pierre Olaf
Chou-Chou	Miiko Taka
Zorgus	Roger C. Carmel
Fromkis	Irving Jacobson
Janitor	Jay Novello
Mrs. Fromkis	Naomi Stevens

Pepe de Winter	Renzo Cesana
Prince	Leon Belasco
Judge	Louis Mercier
Prosecutor	Maurice Marsac
Fanny	Fifi D'Orsay
Executioner	Marcel Hillaire
Couchette	Dawn Villere
Margo	Nan Martin
Yvette	Victoria Carroll
Betti	Sharon Shore
Cerise	Astrid de Brea
Cesar	Emile Genest
Painter	Paul Verdier

Synopsis

Deciding to leave Paris where he has been a conspicuously unsuccessful artist and return to the United States to marry his wealthy fiancée Laurie, Paul meets unexpected opposition from his roommate Casey, a struggling writer. As they walk along the Seine, Casey suggests faking Paul's suicide as a means of creating interest in his paintings and ultimately avoiding a rash marriage. While Casey is occupied with writing the suicide note, Paul swims to the rescue of Nikki, whose virtue is imperilled. Emerging from the water, they find safety on a barge, but Casey, as well as the media, concludes that Paul has perished. As an artist, Paul is honored more in death than in life, and the market for his painting grows to such an extent that he takes refuge in a nightclub to execute enough paintings to meet the demands. Laurie comes to Paris, meets Casey, and captivates him. The jealous Paul decides to get even with his friend by manufacturing evidence that Casey had killed him. Casey is then captured and subjected to the rigor of the French judicial system. Just before Casey's execution by guillotine, Paul saves him.

Commentary

Merman writes, "It was a featherweight comedy that sank like lead. I played a madam. I had lots of gowns and some outrageous wigs, including a pistachio-colored one (**B307**, p. 235)."

F27   *AIRPLANE!*
            (Paramount, 1980; 88 minutes; Video: Paramount Home Video)

Credits

Producer	Jon Davison

Executive producers,
    directors, screen-
    writers
	Jim Abrahams, David Zucker,
	Jerry Zucker

Cinematographer	Joseph Biroc
Designer	Ward Preston
Editor	Patrick Kennedy
Music	Elmer Bernstein
Set	Anne D. McCulley
Costumes	Rosanna Norton

Cast

Murdock	Kareem Abdul-Jabbar
McCroskey	Lloyd Bridges
Captain Oveur	Peter Graves
Elaine	Julie Hagerty
Ted Striker	Robert Hays
Dr. Rumack	Leslie Nielsen
Randy	Lorna Patterson
Kramer	Robert Stack
Johnny	Stephen Stucker
Jive Lady	Barbara Billingsley
Mrs. Davis	Joyce Bulifant
Japanese General	James Hong
Nun	Maureen McGovern
Lt. Hurwitz	**Ethel Merman**
Air Controller Neubauer	Kenneth Tobey
Windshield Wiper Man	Jimmie Walker

Man in Taxi   Howard Jarvis

Synopsis

Striker, an ex-military aviator with a fear of flying, finds himself on a jet liner that develops engine trouble. The entire crew contracts food poisoning, necessitating Striker's taking the controls. Despite his fears, Striker lands the plane successfully with the aid via radio of his former commanding officer.

The film is rich in sight gags and visual humor, including the brief scene in which Merman appears. A hospitalized, delirious serviceman dreams he is Ethel Merman, at which point she rises up from the bed and sings a snatch of "Everything's Coming up Roses."

Review: See **B172**.

F28   *THE WORLD OF TOMORROW*
               (Direct Cinema; 1985; 83, 58, and
               30 minute versions)

Credits

Director   Tom Johnson

Commentary

In this film about the 1939 World's Fair, "The World of Tomorrow," Merman sings "Dawn of a New Day." The date and place of the actual performance has not been determined. It may be 1 January 1939 at Radio City Music Hall when "the dawn of a new day" was proclaimed the official slogan of the fair. Merman, on the other hand, might have been part of the opening festivities on 1 May. Finally, she may have joined the almost endless parade of entertainers who performed throughout the term of the fair.

Stage Appearances

S01   *Keen's English Chop House* (New York; 1929)

Merman worked at this restaurant several times.

S02   *Little Russia* (New York; September 1929)

Earning $60 a week for a two-week engagement, Merman imitated Libby Holman's version of "Moanin' Low," then sang "I've Got a Feeling I'm Falling" and "Little White Lies." Here she was met and signed by agent Lou Irwin.

S03   *Les Ambassadeurs* (New York; October 1929)

Clayton, Jackson, and Durante were the headliners in their own club, but Merman did not work directly with them. In the first part of the show, Merman appeared with the chorus and later did a solo spot featuring "Moanin' Low" and "Body and Soul."

Review: See **B266**.

S04   *Roman Pools Casino* (Miami, FL; 1929)

Recovering from a tonsillectomy, Merman earned $300 per week in support of comedian Joe E. Lewis. "Moanin' Low" was her big number.

S05   *Ritz Theatre* (Elizabeth, NJ; 1930)

Merman and pianist/ arranger Al Siegel broke in their new act at the Ritz.

S06   *Keith's 86th Street Theatre* (New York; 1930)

S07   *Paramount Theatre* (Brooklyn, NY; 1930)

Merman and Siegel, on a bill with the orchestra of Paul Ash, did four or five shows a day for seven weeks.

S08   *Pavilion Royale* (Valley Stream, Long Island, NY; 1930)

The managers of this club presented All-Star Sunday Evening Impromptus, which gave an opportunity to stars to test new material, beginners to appear before sympathetic audiences, and producers to discover talent at all stages of development. In this engagement Merman enjoyed singing with Guy Lombardo's orchestra. Her numbers included "Singin' in the Rain" and "Sing, You Sinners."

S09   *Palace Theatre* (New York; 13 September 1930)

Two-a-day vaudeville was then the fashion at the Palace, the flagship theatre of the Keith circuit. During these appearances, Merman and Siegel performed at the Palace and then raced to the Alvin Theatre to rehearse

Girl Crazy.

Review: See **B332**.

S10   *GIRL CRAZY* (1930)

Credits

Book   Guy Bolton, John MacGowan
Music   George Gershwin
Lyrics   Ira Gershwin
Producers   Alex A. Aarons, Vinton Freedley
Director   Alexander Leftwich
Musical Director   Earl Busby
Choreographer   George Hale
Scenery Designer   Donald Oenslager
Costume Designer   Kiviette

Cast

Danny Churchill   Allen Kearns
Molly Gray   Ginger Rogers
Pete   Clyde Veaux
Lank Sanders   Carlton Macy
Gieber Goldfarb   Willie Howard
Flora James   Eunice Healy
Patsy West   Peggy O'Connor
Kate Fothergill   **Ethel Merman**
Slick Fothergill   William Kent
Sam Mason   Donald Foster
Tess Parker   Olive Brady
Jake Howell   Lew Parker
Eagle Rock   Chief Rivers
Hotel Proprietor   Jack Classon
Lariat Joe   Starr Jones
Sergeant of Police   Norman Curtis
The Foursome   Marshall Smith, Ray Johnson
                       Del Porter, Dwight Snyder

Antonio and Renée De Marco; Red Nichols and
His Orchestra: Roger Edens at the piano

Ladies of the ensemble: Lillian Ostrom, Kay
Downer, Gertrude Lowe, Norma Butler, Gloria

Beaumont, Kathryn Cathcart, Julia Pirie, Vivian Porter, Ruth Gordon, Mary Mascher, Virginia May, Marion Harcke, Muriel La Count, Lillian Loray, Elsie Neal, Faye Greene, Nondas Wayne, Ruth Timmons, La Vern Evans, Betty Morton, Bobby Loyd, Vivian Keefer, Dorothy Donnelly, Jane Lane, Gene Brady, Lillian Garson, Marvyn Ray, Thomasine Haye, Dorothy Gordon, Leila Laney, Paulette Winston, Rena Landeau, Kathy Shauer.

Gentlemen of the ensemble: Bob Gebhardt, Bob Derden, Hazard Newberry, Bob Burton, Harry Griffin, Jack Fago, James Novarro, Starr Jones, Norman Curtis, John Sciortino, Jack Classon, Kendally Northrop, Mickie Forbs, Jack Barrett, Arthur Craig, Dick Nealy.

The Play's History

   Girl Crazy opened on 14 October 1930 at the Alvin Theatre in New York, NY, and ran for 272 performances.
   The play was filmed three times: as *Girl Crazy* (RKO, 1932) with Bert Wheeler and Robert Woolsey; as *Girl Crazy* (MGM, 1943) with Judy Garland and Mickey Rooney; and as *Where the Boys Meet the Girls* (MGM, 1965) with Connie Francis and Harve Presnell.

Synopsis

   Danny Churchill, a wealthy wastrel from New York, upon his father's order settles in Custerville, AZ, notable for its absence of wine, women, and song. Gieber Goldfarb, his taxi driver, accompanies him and becomes the sheriff. Ever dissolute, the bored Churchill opens a dude ranch featuring a gambling casino and imports a bevy of Broadway "chorines." One scrape leads to another, but the love of a good woman reforms Churchill, who falls in love with the postmistress, Molly Gray.

Commentary

In the pit orchestra, conducted by Gershwin himself on opening night, were musical giants-in-the-making, Tommy Dorsey, Jimmy Dorsey, Benny Goodman, Jack Teagarden, Glenn Miller, Gene Krupa, and Joe Venuti, as well as pianist/arranger Roger Edens.

Reviews: See **B12**, **B49**, **B88**, **B288**, **B369**, **B432**, **B458**, **B557**.

S11   *Casino in the Park* (New York; 4 November, 1930; 31 Mar. 1931)

Roger Edens was now Merman's accompanist and arranger, and they shared the bill with Leo Reisman's orchestra and Eddy Duchin at the piano.

S12   *Paramount Theatre* (New York; June 1931)

Johnny Green and Roger Edens accompanied Merman at twin pianos.

Review: See **B158**.

S13   *Palace Theatre* (New York; July 1931)

Merman's numbers were "Sing, You Sinners," "Beyond the Blue Horizon," and "I Got Rhythm." Johnny Green and Roger Edens provided piano accompaniment.

S14   *GEORGE WHITE'S SCANDALS* (11th ed., 1931)

Credits

Sketches	George White, Lew Brown, Irving Caesar
Songs	Lew Brown, Ray Henderson
Producer, Director	George White
Musical Director	Al Goodman
Scenery Designer	Joseph Urban
Costume Designer	Charles Le Maire

Cast

Rudy Vallee	Ross McLean
Everett Marshall	Hazel Boffinger
Ethel Barrymore Colt	Lois Eckhart
Peggy Moseley	Willie & Eugene Howard
Alice Frohman	Gale Quadruplets
Joanna Allen	Barbara Blair
Ethel Merman	Jane Alden
Ray Bolger	Joan Abbott
Loomis Sisters	Fred Manatt

The Most Beautiful Show Girls on the Stage: Hazel Boffinger, Pearl Bradley, Lois Eckhart, Joanna Allen, Peggy Moseley, Renée Johnson, Cornelia Rogers, Mae Slattery, Jacqueline Feeley, Inez Du Plessis, Anne Morgan, Peggy Ring, Julia Gorman, Mary Ann Carr, Patricia Howard, Margaret Heller, Hazel Nevin, Alice Faye, Marian Thompson, Adelaide Raleigh, Ethel Lawrence, Joan English, Myra Gerald, Beth Foth, Betty Allen, Dorothy Daly, Patsy Clarke, Gay Delis, Rose Collins, Dorothy Keene, Gloria Mossman, Hilda Knight, Gloria Pierre, Florence Johnson, Gay Hill.

The Revue's History

George White's Scandals opened on 14 September 1931 at the Apollo Theatre, New York, NY, and ran for 202 performances.

Commentary

Merman's songs were "Life Is Just a Bowl of Cherries," "Ladies and Gentlemen, That's Love," "My Song," and "The Good Old Days."

Reviews: See **B23**, **B168**, **B215**, **B287**, **B370**.

S15 *Casino in the Park* (New York; January 1932)

Merman sang with Leo Reisman's orchestra with Eddy Duchin at the piano.

S16 *Palace Theatre* (New York; 24 April 1932)

Merman's numbers included "Smile, Darn You, Smile" and "There'll Be Some Changes Made" with "I Got Rhythm" and "Life Is Just a Bowl of Cherries" as encores. Roger Edens and Jack Carroll provided piano accompaniment.

Review: See **B552**.

S17 *HUMPTY DUMPTY* (1932)

Credits

Book	B. G. De Sylva, Lawrence Schwab
Additional Dialogue	Sid Silvers
Songs	Nacio Herb Brown
	Richard A. Whiting
Producers	Laurence Schwab, B. G. De Sylva
Director	Laurence Schwab
Musical Director	Lou Silvers
Choreographer	George Hale
Scenery Designers	Cleon Throckmorton
	Charles Le Maire
Costume Designer	Kiviette

Cast

Sam Moscow	Lou Holtz
Rebecca Moscowitz	Lisa Silvert
Louis Mosco	Sid Silvers
Consuelo	Doris Groday
D. W. Croffuth	Douglas Wood
Martin Sully	Eddie Foy, Jr.
Michael Sully	J. C. Nugent
Gerald Townsend	William Lynn
Irene Parker	June Knight
Wanda Brill	**Ethel Merman**
Bonelli	Walter Armen
Peter Knox	Harry T. Shannon
Jay Gordon	Oscar Ragland
Miss Jersey City	Sara Jane
Dancer	Vernon Biddle
Show Girl	Toni Chase
Actress	Edith Speare
Steve	O. J. Banasse
The Diamond Boys	Tom, Harold, Hugh Diamond
Mary and Bobby	Mary and Bobby Day
The Admirals	Thomas Ladd, Jack Armstrong, Budd Kehlner, Paul Pegue
The Ritz Quartette	Edward Delbridge, Neil Evans, Chet Bree, William H. Stamm

Dancers: Gene Brady, Jean Carson, Dody Donnelly, Madeline Dunbar, Mitzi Garner, Billy Green, Frances Gordon, Marion Herson, Juliette Jenner, Dorothy Kal, Irene Kelly, Evelyn Laurie, Frances McHugh, Florence Mallee, Mary Joan Martin, Peggy Moseley, Ann McKenney, Bernice O'Neal, Blanche Poston, Julia Pirie, Adelaide Raleigh, Llona Sears, Marie Vannerman, Leona Wallace, Mildred Webb, Betty Allen

The Play's History

Humpty Dumpty opened on 26 September 1932 at the Nixon Theatre, Pittsburgh, PA, and closed there.

Synopsis

Merman called the script an "ambitious satiric survey of American history cast in the form of a Broadway revue (**B307**, p. 57)."

Review: See **B372**.

S18   *TAKE A CHANCE* (1932)

Credits

Book	B. G. De Sylva, Laurence Schwab
Additional Dialogue	Sid Silvers
Songs	Nacio Herb Brown, Richard Whiting
Additional Songs	Vincent Youmans
Producers	Laurence Schwab, B. G. De Sylva
Director	Edgar MacGregor
Musical Director	Max Meth
Musical Numbers	Bobby Connolly
Scenery Designer	Cleon Throckmorton
Costume Designers	Kiviette, Charles Le Maire

Cast

Duke Stanley	Jack Haley
Louie Webb	Sid Silvers
Toni Ray	June Knight
Wanda Brill	**Ethel Merman**
Kenneth Raleigh	Jack Whiting
Andrew Raleigh	Douglas Wood
Consuelo Raleigh	Mitzi Mayfair
Mike Caruso	Robert Gleckler
Thelma Green	Josephine Dunn
A Butler	George Pauncefort
The Ritz Quartette	William H. Stamm, Edward Delbridge, Neil Evans, Chet Bree
The Admirals	Tommy Ladd, Jack Armstrong, Budd Kehlner, Paul Pegue

Actors and actresses in Kenneth Raleigh's Revue *Humpty Dumpty*: Oscar Ragland, Sara Jane,

John Grant, Louise Seidel, Lee Beggs, Al Downing, Andrew and Louise Carr.

Dancers: Louise Allen, Gerry Billings, Lucille Brodin, Flo Brooks, Jean Carson, Marian Dixon, Helen Fairweather, Emily Fitzpatrick, Arline Garfield, Frances Gordon, Ethel Green, Marion Herson, Julie Jenner, Dorothy Kal, Gloria Kelly, Paula King, Jane Lane, Evelyn Laurie, Florence Mallee, Anna Marie McKenney, Frances McHugh, Dorothy Morgan, Julia Pirie, Blanche Poston, Adelaide Raleigh, Mildred Webb, James Ardell, Henry King, Clark Leston, Edward Shane

The Play's History

   Take a Chance opened on 26 November 1932 at the Apollo Theatre, New York, NY, and ran for 243 performances. When it was filmed by Paramount in 1933, the stars were Lillian Roth, June Knight, James Dunn, and Cliff Edwards.

Synopsis

   After being attracted to show business by participating in a production of the Hasty Pudding Club at Harvard, Kenneth Raleigh decides to produce a Broadway musical. Unfortunately, he encounters two slicksters, Duke Stanley and Louie Webb, who are promoting the career of Toni Ray. Raleigh and Ray fall in love.

Commentary

   Merman's four songs were "You're an Old Smoothie," "I Got Religion," "Rise and Shine," and "Eadie Was a Lady."

Reviews: See **B21**, **B61**, **B75**, **B217**, **B277**, **B291**, **B371**, **B373**, **B419**, **B577**.

S19   *Paramount Theatre* (New York; September 1933)

Review: See **B549**.

S20   *Paramount Theatre* (New York; 27 April 1934)

Merman's songs included "Love Thy Neighbor" and "Eadie Was a Lady."

Reviews: See **B550**, **B551**.

S21   *ANYTHING GOES* (1934)

Credits

Book	P. G. Wodehouse, Guy Bolton
Book Revision	Howard Lindsay, Russel Crouse
Music and Lyrics	Cole Porter
Producer	Vinton Freedley
Director	Howard Lindsay
Musical Director	Earl Busby
Choreographer	Robert Alton
Scenery Designer	Donald Oenslager
Costume Designer	Jenkins

Cast

Bartender	George E. Mack
Elisha J. Whitney	Paul Everton
Billy Crocker	William Gaxton
Bellboy	Irving Pincus
Reno Sweeney	**Ethel Merman**
Reporter	Edward Delbridge
First Cameraman	Chet Bree
Second Cameraman	Neal Evans
Sir Evelyn Oakleigh	Leslie Barrie
Hope Harcourt	Bettina Hall
Mrs. Wadsworth T. Harcourt	Helen Raymond
Bishop Dodson	Pacie Ripple
Ching	Richard Wang
Ling	Charlie Fang
Snooks	Drucilla Strain

Steward	William Stamm
Assistant Purser	Val Vestoff
First Federal Man	Harry Wilson
Second Federal Man	Arthur Imperato
Mrs. Wentworth	May Abbey
Mrs. Frick	Florence Earle
Reverend Dr. Moon	Victor Moore
Bonnie Letour	Vera Dunn
Chief Officer	Houston Richards
Ship's Drunk	William Barry
Mr. Swift	Maurice Elliott
Little Boy	Billy Curtis
Captain	John C. King
Babe	Vivian Vance
The Foursome	Marshall Smith, Ray Johnson, Dwight Snyder, Del Porter
The Ritz Quartette	Chet Bree, Bill Stamm, Neal Evans, Ed Delbridge
The Alvin Quartette	Arthur Imperato, David Glidden, Richard Nealy, Stuart Fraser
Ship's Orchestra	The Stylists

Reno's Angels: Ruth Bond, Norma Butler, Enes Early, Marjorie Fisher, Ruth Gomley, Irene Hamlin, Renée Johnson, Irene Kelly, Leoda Knapp, Doris Maye, Lilliam Ostrom, Jackie Paige, Mary Philips, Cornelia Rogers, Frances Stewart, Ruth Shaw, Eleanore Sheridan

The Play's History

    Anything Goes opened on 21 November 1934 at the Alvin Theatre, New York, NY, and ran for 420 performances.

    Its premiere in London occurred on 14 June 1935 at the Palace Theatre, with Sydney Howard, Peter Haddon, Jack Whiting, Adele Dixon, and Jeanne Aubert. The show lasted for 261 performances.

    Revivals were seen in New York in 1962 (239 performances) as an off-Broadway production and in 1987 at Lincoln Center.

Revivals were mounted in London on 18 November 1969 and July 1989.

Anything Goes was filmed twice: in 1936, with Merman and Bing Crosby, and in 1956, with Mitzi Gaynor and Bing Crosby.

Synopsis

Cabaret singer Reno Sweeney, about to embark for Europe, is in love with Billy Crocker, who boards the ship to say farewell to Hope Harcourt, his former fiancée. Their encounter convinces Crocker that he still loves Harcourt, so he remains on board after the ship sails. Crocker obtains a ticket and a passport from the Rev. Dr. Moon, who is really Public Enemy No. 13 in flight from the law; they had belonged to an accomplice who failed to appear, so Crocker is invited to pretend to be Moon's associate. As a result, Crocker encounters both Harcourt and Sweeney as himself and others as Moon's ally, which leads to great confusion. When the captain learns that a criminal is aboard his ship, he instigates a search and locks up the felon, after which he invites the passengers to unburden their souls in true evangelistic style.

Harcourt has gone to England to marry Sir Evelyn Oakleigh, not for love, but for money to save the family business. She learns, however, that the business has been profitably sold, so she is free to marry Crocker. Sweeney's loss is assuaged by the romantic interest of Oakleigh.

Commentary

Porter fashioned songs for Merman that demonstrated the range of her talent: "You're the Top," "Anything Goes," "Buddy, Beware," "Blow, Gabriel, Blow," and "I Get a Kick out of You."

Reviews: See **B13**, **B50**, **B166**, **B170**, **B180**, **B216**, **B239**, **B286**, **B486**, **B581**.

S22   *Paramount Theatre* (New York; 11 April 1936)

S23   *RED, HOT, AND BLUE!* (1936)

Credits

Book	Howard Lindsay, Russel Crouse
Music and Lyrics	Cole Porter
Producer	Vinton Freedley
Director	Howard Lindsay
Musical Director	Frank Tours
Choreographer	George Hale
Scenery Designer	Donald Oenslager
Costume Designer	Constance Ripley

Cast

Reporters	Geoffrey Errett, Kark Kohrs, Bill Houston, Norman Lind, Vivian Vance, Betty Allen
Deputy Warden	Lew Parker
Warden of Lark's Nest Prison	Forrest Orr
"Nails" O'Reilly Duquesne	**Ethel Merman**
"Policy" Pinkle	Jimmy Durante
Vivian	Vivian Vance
Anne Westcott	Dorothy Vernon
Grace	Grace Hartman
Lucille	Lucille Johnson
Cecile	Cecile Carey
Kay	Kay Picture
Irene	Ethelyne Holt
Betty	Betty Allen
"Fingers"	Paul Hartman
Bob Hale	Bob Hope
Sonny Hadley	Thurston Crane
Peaches La Fleur	Polly Walters
"Ratface" Dugan	Bill Benner
"Sure Thing" Simpson	Prentiss Davis
"Flap-Ears" Metelli	Leo Shippers
"Louie the Louse"	Bernard Jannsen

Mrs. Peabody	May Abbey
Tiny	Anne Wolfe
Louella	Jeanette Owens
Senator Musilovitch	Lew Parker
Senator Malvinsky	Robert Leonard
Senator O'Shaughnessy	Forrest Orr
Senator Del Grasso	Houston Richards
Sergeant-at-Arms	Norman Lind
First Expressman	Geoffrey Errett
Second Expressman	Karl Kohrs
Girl	Gloria Clare
First Marine	Frank Archer
Second Marine	Bruce Covert
Decorator	Houston Richards

The Play's History

Red, Hot, and Blue! opened on 29 October 1936 at the Alvin Theatre, New York, NY, and ran for 183 performances. Betty Hutton starred in the film, released by Paramount in 1949.

Synopsis

Merman described the very slight story: "A Washington matron (me) was conducting a lottery which was to be run by an ex-convict (Jimmy Durante) and won by a lawyer (Bob Hope) whom I loved, but who was hung up on the memory of a broad (Polly Walters) who as a baby had branded her behind by sitting on a waffle iron (**B307**, p. 80)."

Commentary

"Down in the Depths on the 90th Floor," "Ridin' High," "You're a Bad Influence on Me," "Red, Hot, and Blue," and "It's De-Lovely" were Merman's songs, the last a duet sung with Bob Hope. She later observed, *"Red, Hot and Blue* [sic] was in no way innovative. It wasn't even a slick old-fashioned show. But in a day when audiences were content to settle for star turns, it did very nicely for Jimmy, Bob and me (**B307**, p. 83)."

Reviews: See **B09**, **B25**, **B60**, **B90**, **B258**, **B275**, **B290**, **B433**, **B568**, **B582**.

S24   *Gershwin Memorial Concert* (New York: Lewisohn Stadium; 9 August 1937)

Numerous artists, including Merman, performed in this concert in honor of the recently deceased George Gershwin. Merman sang three of Gershwin's songs, including "I Got Rhythm." There was a second memorial concert on 12 July, but Merman did not participate.

Reviews: See **B173**, **B326**.

S25   *Strand Theatre* (New York; September 1938)

S26   *STARS IN YOUR EYES* (1939)

Credits

Book	J. P. McEvoy
Music	Arthur Schwartz
Lyrics	Dorothy Fields
Producer	Dwight Deere Wiman
Director	Joshua Logan
Musical Director	Al Goodman
Choreographer	Carl Randall
Scenery Designer	Jo Mielziner
Costume Designer	John Hambleton

Cast

Assistant Director	Ted Gary
Second Assistant Director	Davis Cunningham
Third Assistant Director	Edward Kane
Fourth Assistant Director	Robert Shanley
Fifth Assistant Director	Dan Dailey, Jr.
Sixth Assistant Director	Roger Stearns

First Girl	Edith Grant
Second Girl	Thekla Horn
Third Girl	Nancy Wiman
Wardrobe Woman	Johanne Hoven
Carpenter	David Morris
Fourth Girl	Frances Rands
Electrician	Anthony Albert
Soundman	Rennie McEvoy
Babe	Dawn Roland
Wilder	Clinton Sundberg
Cameraman	Walter Wagner
Assistant Soundman	Ambrose Costello
Fifth Girl	Phyllis Roque
Sixth Girl	Natasha Dana
Dancing Girl	Nora Kaye
Leading Man	Walter Cassel
Script Girl	Gloria Clare
Jeanette Adair	**Ethel Merman**
Bess	Mildred Natwick
Voice Coach	Mary Wickes
Maid	Kathryn Mayfield
Jockey	Basil Galahoff
Bill	Jimmy Durante
Darrow	Robert Ross
John Blake	Richard Carlson
Tata	Tamara Toumanova
Dawson	Richard Barbee
Photographers	Walter Cassel, Edward Kane, Davis Cunningham, Robert Shanley
Russian Consul	Russel Protopoff
French Consul	Dwight Godwin
Italian Consul	Fernando Alonso
English Consul	David Morris
German Consul	Ambrose Costello
Watchman	Ambrose Costello

Ladies and Gentlemen of the Ballet: Alicia Alonso, Peggy Conrad, Maria De Galanta, Jane Everett, Gail Grant, Marion Haynes, Thekla Horn, Johanne Hoven, Marjorie Johnstone, Nora Kaye, Maria Karniloff, Frances Rands, Audrey Reynolds, Olga Suarez, Margaret Vasilieff, Mary Jane Williams, Anthony Albert, Fernando Alonso, Paul Alvin, Sayva Andreieff, Dwight

Godwin, Basil Galahoff, George Kiddon, Russel
Protopoff, Richard Reed, Newcombe Rice, Jerome
Robbins

The Play's History

   Stars in Your Eyes opened at the Majestic
Theatre, New York, NY, on 9 February 1939, and
ran for 127 performances.

Synopsis

   Jeanette Adair (Merman) is a star who has
inherited Monotonous Pictures from her deceased producer husband. She falls in love
with her leftist director, whose interest is
in a Russian waif whose career he tries to advance at the expense of Jeanette's.

Commentary

   Merman writes that her character was "as
grand as Norma Shearer, as tough as Carole
Lombard and as pampered as Joan Crawford, with
a coach (Mary Wickes) following [her] with a
Victrola playing atmospheric music to get me
in the mood. . . . It was my best shot at
acting yet (**B307**, p. 100)."

Reviews: See **B10**, **B26**, **B130**, **B156**, **B182**,
B259, **B276**, **B376**, **B455**, **B553**, **B559**, **B569**,
B583.

S27   *DU BARRY WAS A LADY* (1939)

Credits

Book   Herbert Fields, B. G. De Sylva
Songs   Cole Porter
Producer   B. G. De Sylva
Director   Edgar MacGregor
Musical Director   Gene Salzer
Choreographer   Robert Alton
Scen./Costume Designer   Raoul Pene Du Bois

Cast

Jones	Hugh Cameron
Bill Kelly	Walter Armin
Harry Norton	Charles Walters
Alice Barton	Betty Grable
Florian	Harold Cromer
Louis Blore	Bert Lahr
Vi Hennessey	Jean Moorehead
May Daley	**Ethel Merman**
Alex Barton	Ronald Graham
Ann Barton	Kay Sutton
Manuel Gomez	Tito Renaldo
Charley	Benny Baker
Four Internationals	Douglas Hawkins,

Peter Holliday, Robert Herring, Carl Nicholas

Starlets of the Club Petit: Geraldine Spreckels, Betty Allen, Ann Graham, Janice Carter, Jacqueline Franc, Marguerite Benton

Dancing Girls: Stella Clauson, Nina Wayler, Marion Harvey, Tilda Getze, Nancy Knott, Jane Sproule, Helen Bennett, Edyth Turgell, Barbara Pond, Evelyn Bonefine, Ruth Bond, Patricia Knight, Adele Jergens, Frances Krell, Gloria Martin, Beverly Hosier, Gloria Arden, Marie Vannemen, Virginia Cheneval

Dancing Boys: Gene Ashley, Boris Butleroff, Joel Friend, Russel Georgiev, Stanley Grill, Mel Kacher, Don Liberto, Tito Renaldo, Lewis Turner, Paul Thorne.

The Play's History

Du Barry Was a Lady opened on 6 December 1939 at the 46th Street Theatre, New York, NY, and ran for 408 performances.

Its London premiere occurred on 22 Oct. 1942 at His Majesty's Theatre, with Arthur Riscoe, Jackie Hunter, Bruce Trent, Frances

Day, Inga Anderson, and Bud Flanagan in the leading roles.

It was filmed in 1943 with Lucille Ball, Gene Kelly, and Red Skelton.

Synopsis

May Daley, an exuberant cabaret singer, is pursued by an ardent washroom attendant, Louis Blore. When he wins $75,000, Blore hopes to impress Daley by buying the club. Daley, alas, loves Alex Barton. Blore's plan to incapacitate Barton backfires when Blore himself drinks a doctored cocktail he intended for Barton.

In his stupor Blore dreams that he is Louis XIV in pursuit of Madame du Barry, who is a mirror image of May Daley. Blore is much more successful in his dream than in his waking moments, but his passion is considerably dampened by an errant arrow shot by the imbecilic dauphin into the king's privates.

Blore awakens and decides to give Barton $10,000 so he can marry Daley. Taxes claim the remainder of his money, so Blore resumes his work as washroom attendant.

Commentary

Merman observed, "It was what we used to call a tired-businessman's entertainment. In fact, the critics felt the situation would have suited a burlesque show if everything hadn't been first class--the writing, songs, cast, direction, scenery, costumes--everything (**B307**, p. 106)."

Reviews: See **B22**, **B55**, **B183**, **B260**, **B274**, **B329**, **B518**, **B554**, **B566**, **B571**.

S28   *PANAMA HATTIE* (1940)

Credits

Book	Herbert Fields, B. G. De Sylva
Songs	Cole Porter
Producer	B. G. De Sylva
Director	Edgar MacGregor
Musical Director	Gene Salzer
Choreographer	Robert Alton
Scen./Cost. Designer	Raoul Pene Du Bois

Cast

Mrs. Gonzales	Conchita
Mac	Eppy Pearson
Skat Briggs	Pat Harrington
Windy Deegan	Frank Hyers
Woozy Hogan	Rags Ragland
Chiquita	Nadine Gae
Fruit Peddler	Linda Griffith
Tim	Roger Gerry
Tom	Roy Blaine
Ted	Ted Daniels
Ty	Lipman Duckat
Hattie Maloney	**Ethel Merman**
Leila Tree	Phyllis Brooks
Mildred Hunter	Elaine Shepard
Kitty Belle Randolph	Ann Graham
Nick Bullett	James Dunn
Florrie	Betty Hutton
Geraldine Bullett	Joan Carroll
Vivian Budd	Arthur Treacher
First Stranger	Hal Conklin
Second Stranger	Frank De Ross
Mike	Jack Donahue
Whitney Randolph	James Kelso

Singing Girls: Janis Carter, Ann Graham, Marguerite Benton, Vera Dean

Dancing Girls: June Allyson, Irene Austin, Jane Ball, Mimi Berry, Betsy Blair, Lucille Bremer, Nancy Chaplin, Kathryn Coulter, Ronnie

Cunningham, Marianne Crude, Doris Dowling, Vera-Ellen, Miriam Franklyn, Marguerite James, Pat Likely, Mary McDonald, Renée Russell, Audrey Westphal

Dancing Boys: Jack Baker, Cliff Ferre, Fred Ney, Harry Rogue, Jack Riley, Billy Skipper, Art Stanley, Carl Trees, Don Weismuller

The Play's History

Panama Hattie opened on 30 October 1940 at the 46th Street Theatre, New York, NY, and ran for 501 performances.

Bebe Daniels starred as Hattie in the London production, which opened at the Piccadilly Theatre on 4 Nov. 1944.

MGM made a cinematic version of the play in 1942 with Ann Sothern, but it bears little resemblance to the original.

Synopsis

Brassy Hattie Maloney owns the Tropical Shore Bar in the Panama Canal Zone. She decides to become refined enough to merit the attention of socialite diplomat Nick Bullett. When Maloney and Bullett decide to be married, she insists that Bullett's daughter Geraldine ought to be consulted. Geraldine, who has been reared as a gentlewoman, is at first shocked by Maloney's speech and dress; she is not disposed to approve the marriage. Luckily, Maloney overhears a plot to dynamite the Canal, and with the assistance of three sailor friends, she foils the attempt. When Geraldine sees that Maloney is a heroine, she relents, thus allowing the marriage.

Commentary

Of her character, Merman wrote, "Hattie Maloney was an expansion of the Katie Who Went to Haiti. Only Hattie had the capacity to grow. In fact, she was quite a dame. Hattie was a brassy broad who hung out with sailors and didn't speak correct, but she had a softer side (**B307**, p. 112)."

Reviews: See **B24**, **B184**, **B289**, **B513**, **B555**, **B567**, **B572**, **B584**.

S29   *SOMETHING FOR THE BOYS* (1943)

Credits

Book	Herbert and Dorothy Fields
Songs	Cole Porter
Producer	Michael Todd
Director	Hassard Short
Book Director	Herbert Fields
Musical Director	William Parson
Choreographer	Jack Cole
Scenery Designer	Howard Bay
Costume Designer	Billy Livingston

Cast

Chiquita Hart	Paula Laurence
Roger Calhoun	Jed Prouty
Harry Hart	Allen Jenkins
Blossom Hart	**Ethel Merman**
Staff Sgt. Rocky Fulton	Bill Johnson
Sgt. Laddie Green	Stuart Langley
Mary-Frances	Betty Garrett
Betty-Jean	Betty Bruce
Michaela	Anita Alvarez
Lois and Lucille	Barnes Twins
Lt. Col. S. D. Drubbs	Jack Hartley
Mr. Tobias Twitch	William Lynn
MP	Mervyn Vye
Corp. Burns	Bill Callahan
Sgt. Carter	Remi Martel
Melanie Walker	Frances Mercer
Burke	Walter Rinner
Mrs. Grubbs	Madeleine Clive
Gordon	Alan Fleming

Dancing Girls: Alice Anthony, May Block, Jean Coyne, Betty Deane, Patricia Dearing, Ruth Godfrey, Dolores (Dody) Goodman, Betty Heather, Margie Jackson, Jean Owens, Leslie Shannon, Ethel Sherman, Puddy Smith, Patricia Welles, Helen Wenzel, June Wieting, Nina Starkey

Dancing Boys: Stanley Catron, Bob Davis, Benny De Sio, Jerry Florio, Albert Gaeta, Aaron Gobetz, Ray Harrison, David Mann, Remi Martel, Paul Martin, Duncan Noble, Ricky Riccardi, William Vaux, Joe Viggiano, William Weber, Lou Wills, Jr., Parker Wilson

Singing Boys: Jimmy Allison, Joseph Bell, Alan Fleming, Richard Harvey, Art Lambert, Buddy Irving, Bruce Lord, Paul Mario, John W. Maye, Joseph Monte, Walter Rinner, Mervyn Vye

The Play's History

Something for the Boys opened on 7 January 1943, at the Alvin Theatre, New York, NY, and ran for 422 performances.

Synopsis

Three cousins--Blossom Hart, Chiquita Hart, Harry Hart--discover that they have jointly inherited a four-hundred-acre ranch in Texas. Despite their mutual dislike, they decide to get along in order to be awarded the inheritance. When they go to their ranch, they discover that it is ramshackle and inhabited by men from a nearby airfield, one of whom, Rocky Fulton, was a bandleader in civilian life. Although Blossom is immediately attracted to Fulton, she has a serious rival in Melanie Walker.

Blossom decides to aid the war effort by making part of the ranchhouse a home for servicemen's wives and another a defense factory. Walker surreptitiously tells the base's commanding officer that the ranch is a house of prostitution, which seems to be true when he sees men going in and out of the house and women scantily clad (actually they have taken showers after their day's work in the factory). Accordingly, the ranch is declared off limits to the flyers.

At this low point in her fortunes, Blossom discovers that she is a radio receiver because of her carborundum dental fillings. Even the base commander finds this interesting because each serviceman can be a radio receiver. He becomes Blossom's friend when she uses her radio teeth to save a plane in distress; now she has no trouble convincing him that her ranch is legitimate. Naturally, Blossom and Fulton are united in the end.

Commentary

Merman sang, in addition to the title song, "When We're Home on the Range," "Hey, Good Lookin'," "He's a Right Guy," "The Leader of a Big Time Band," "There's a Happy Land in the Sky," and a duet, "By the Mississinewa."

Reviews: See **B175, B181, B335, B442, B514, B519, B557, B585.**

S30   *ANNIE GET YOUR GUN*   (1946)

Credits

Book	Herbert and Dorothy Fields
Songs	Irving Berlin
Producers	Richard Rodgers, Oscar Hammerstein II
Director	Joshua Logan
Musical Director	Jay Blackton
Choreographer	Helen Tamiris
Scenery Designer	Jo Mielziner
Costume Designer	Lucinda Ballard

Cast

Little Boy	Warren Berlinger
Little Girl	Mary Ellen Glass
Charlie Davenport	Marty May
Iron Tail	Daniel Nagrin
Yellow Foot	Walter John
Mac	Cliff Dunstan
Cowboys	Rob Taylor, Bernard Griffin, Jack Pierce
Cowgirls	Mary Grey, Franca Baldwin
Foster Wilson	Art Barnett
Coolie	Beau Tilden
Dolly Tate	Lea Penman
Winnie Tate	Betty Anne Nyman
Tommy Keeler	Kenny Bowers
Frank Butler	Ray Middleton
Girl with Bouquet	Katrina Van Oss
Annie Oakley	**Ethel Merman**
Minnie	Nancy Jean Raab
Jessie	Camilla De Witt
Nellie	Marlene Cameron
Little Jake	Clifford Sales
Harry	Don Liberto
Mary	Ellen Hanley
Buffalo Bill	William O'Neal
Mrs. Little Horse	Alma Ross
Mrs. Black Tooth	Elizabeth Malone
Mrs. Yellow Foot	Nellie Ranson
Trainman	John Garth III
Waiter	Leon Bibb
Porter	Clyde Turner
Riding Mistress	Lubov Roudenko
Pawnee Bill	George Lipton
Chief Sitting Bull	Harry Bellaver
Mabel	Mary Woodley
Louise	Ostrid Lind
Nancy	Dorothy Richards
Timothy Gardner	Jack Bryon
Andy Turner	Earl Sauvain
Clyde Smith	Victor Clarke
John	Rob Taylor
Freddie	Robert Dixon
Wild Horse	Daniel Nagrin

Pawnee's Messenger	Milton Watson
Major Domo	John Garth III
Waiters	Clyde Turner, Leon Bibb
Mr. Schuyler Adams	Don Liberto
Mrs. Schuyler Adams	Dorothy Richards
Dr. Percy Ferguson	Bernard Griffin
Mrs. Percy Ferguson	Marietta Vore
Debutante	Ruth Vrana
Mr. Ernest Henderson	Art Barnett
Mrs. Ernest Henderson	Truly Barbara
Sylvia Potter-Porter	Marjorie Crossland
Mr. Clay	Rob Taylor
Mr. Lockwood	Fred Rivett
Girl in Pink	Christina Lind
Girl in White	Mary Grey

Singers and Dancers: Truly Barbara, Ellen Hanley, Christina Lind, Ostrid Lind, Dorothy Richards, Ruth Strickland, Katrina Van Oss, Marietta Vore, Ruth Vrana, Mary Woodley, Jack Bryon, Victor Clarke, Robert Dixon, Bernard Griffin, Marvin Goodis, Vincent Henry, Don Liberto, Fred Rivett, Earl Sauvain, Rob Taylor, Franca Baldwin, Tessie Carrano, Madeleine Detry, Cuprienne Gabelman, Barbara Gaye, Evelyn Giles, Mary Grey, Harriet Roeder, Jack Beaber, John Begg, Michael Maule, Duncan Noble, Jack Pierce, Paddy Stone, Ken Whelan, Parker Wilson

The Play's History

Annie Get Your Gun opened on 16 May 1946 at the Imperial Theatre, New York, NY, and ran for 1,147 performances.

Its London premiere occurred on 7 June 1947 at the Coliseum Theatre with Dolores Gray as Annie. The show ran for 1,304 performances.

MGM filmed *Annie Get Your Gun* in 1950. Judy Garland, the original star, was replaced by Betty Hutton.

Synopsis

Annie Oakley, an unrefined but winsome backwoodswoman, meets sharpshooter Frank Butler when he appears in Cincinnati with Pawnee Bill's Wild West Show. She is immediately smitten by his good looks but realizes that she is not his ideal woman. When Oakley demonstrates that she, too, is a sharpshooter, she also goes into show business as a member of Buffalo Bill's troupe and proves to be excellent competition to Butler. Their romance waxes and wanes, as does their rivalry. When Buffalo Bill and Pawnee Bill combine their shows, the last impediment to Oakley and Butler's attachment is dashed when the competing shows are merged. It is clear, though, that their rivalry will continue.

Commentary

According to Merman, the writers "made this diamond in the rough a full-rounded full-fledged woman. She was a character who demanded I act as well as sing (B307, p. 140)." Her director, Joshua Logan, had already dubbed her "Sarah Bernhardt, Jr."

Reviews: See B33, B38, B56, B58, B59, B167, B178, B225, B300, B324, B436, B497, B515, B516, B520, B586.

S31   *CALL ME MADAM* (1950)

Credits

Book	Howard Lindsay, Russel Crouse
Songs	Irving Berlin
Producer	Leland Hayward
Director	George Abbott
Musical Director	Jay Blackton
Choreographer	Jerome Robbins
Scen./Cost. Designer	Raoul Pene Du Bois
Miss Merman's Costumes	Mainbocher

Cast

Mrs. Sally Adams	**Ethel Merman**
The Secretary of State	Geoffrey Lumb
Supreme Court Justice	Owen Coll
Congressman Wilkins	Pat Harrington
Henry Gibson	William David
Kenneth Gibson	Russell Nype
Senator Gallagher	Ralph Chambers
Secretary to Mrs. Adams	Jeanne Bal
Butler	William Hail
Senator Brockbank	Jay Velie
Cosmo Constantine	Paul Lukas
Pemberton Sebastian	Alan Hewitt
Clerk	Stowe Phelps
Hugo Tantinnin	E. A. Krumschmidt
Sebastian Sebastian	Henry Lascoe
Princess Maria	Galina Talva
Court Chamberlain	William David
A Maid	Lily Paget
Grand Duchess Sophie	Lilia Skala
Grand Duke Otto	Owen Coll

Principal Dancers: Tommy Rall, Muriel Bentley, Arthur Partington, Norma Kaiser

The Potato Bugs: Ollie Engebretson, Richard Fjellman

Singers: Rae Abruzzo, Jeanne Bal, Trudy De Luz, Lydia Fredericks, Estelle Gardner, Ruth McVayne, Lily Paget, Noella Peloquin, Helene Whitney, Aristide Bartis, Nathaniel Frey, William Hail, Albert Linville, Robert Penn, Tom Reider, Joan Sheehan, Stanley Simmonds, Ray Stephens

Dancers: Shellie Farrell, Nina Frenkin, Patricia Hammerlee, Barbara Heath, Norma Kaiser, Virginia Le Roy, Kirsten Valbor, Fred Hearn, Allan Knolls, Kenneth Le Roy, Ralph Linn, Douglas Moppert, Arthur Partington, Bobby Tucker, William Weslow

The Play's History

   Call Me Madam opened on 12 October 1950
at the Imperial Theatre, New York, NY, and ran
for 644 performances.
   In London, Billie Worth played Sally
Adams when the play opened at the Coliseum
Theatre on 15 March 1952.
   The play was filmed in 1953 (Twentieth
Century-Fox) with Merman as Sally Adams.

Synopsis

   Sally Adams, a socialite famous for her
lavish parties, is named ambassadress to Lichtenburg, a tiny, impoverished European prin-
cipality. The Lichtenburgian cabinet, taking
advantage of the lack of diplomatic experience
of Adams, empowers a reluctant Cosmo Constantin, the handsome prime minister, to charm
Adams out of a loan of $100,000,000. Adams, on
the other hand, has been briefed to be wary of
any attempts to borrow money. Meeting Constantin, she almost immediately falls in love with
him and the kingdom and offers the loan. Constantin, on the other hand, wishes his country
to help itself without external intervention
and so refuses the loan. As a result, she is
recalled to Washington where she gives one of
her famous parties. To her surprise and delight, Constantin, now the ambassador to the
U. S., appears in the ballroom, leaving the
romance free to prosper.

Commentary

   "By our opening on October 12," Merman
wrote, "we had racked up the largest advance
sale in the history of the American theatre.
Happily my contract gave me 10 percent of all
profits from the Broadway production, road
companies, movie sale and subsidiary rights
(**B307**, p. 165)."

Reviews: See B20, B34, B37, B62, B70, B71, B107, B169, B177, B235, B253, B256, B294, B318, B334, B437, B438, B439, B517, B521, B587.

S32　　　*They Like Ike* (New York; Madison Square Garden; 8 February 1952)

Merman joined Mary Martin, Clark Gable, Irving Berlin, and other stars in this fund-raiser to support the presidential candidacy of Dwight D. Eisenhower. "There's No Business Like Show Business" was Merman's offering.

S33　　　*The Ethel Merman Show* (Texas State Fair; October 1953)

Roger Edens provided Merman a staple of her subsequent repertory in "I'm Just a Lady with a Song." The ten-day stint included Russell Nype, George Murphy, the Wiere Brothers, and the Harmonica Rascals.

S34　　　*Royal Command Variety Performance* (London; Palladium Theatre; 7 November 1955)

S35　　　*HAPPY HUNTING* (1956)

Credits

Book	Howard Lindsay, Russel Crouse
Music	Harold Karr
Lyrics	Matt Dubey
Producer	Jo Mielziner
Director	Abe Burrows
Musical Director	Jay Blackton
Choreographers	Alex Romero, Bob Herget
Scenery Designer	Jo Mielziner
Costume Designer	Irene Sharaff

Cast

Sanford Stewart, Jr.　　　　　　Gordon Polk

Mrs. Sanford Stewart, Jr.	Olive Templeton
Joseph	Mitchell M. Gregg
Beth Livingstone	Virginia Gibson
Jack Adams	Seth Riggs
Harry Watson	Gene Wesson
Charley	Delbert Anderson
Liz Livingstone	**Ethel Merman**
Sam	Clifford Fearl
Joe	John Craig
Freddy	George Martin
Wes	Jim Hutchison
Mary Mills	Estelle Parsons
Dick Davis	Robert C. Held
Bob Grayson	Carl Nicholas
Maude Foley	Mary Finney
Police Sergeant	Mark Zeller
Arturo	Leon Belasco
The Duke of Granada	Fernando Lamas
Count Carlos	Renato Cibelli
Waiter	Don Weissmuller
Ship's Officer	John Leslie
Barman	Warren J. Brown
Mrs. B.	Florence Dunlap
Mrs. D.	Madeleine Clive
Mrs. L.	Kelley Stephens
Terence	Jim Hutchison
Tom	Eugene Louis
Daisy	Mary Roche
Mr. T., a Member of the Hunt	John Leslie
Mr. M., a Member of the Hunt	Jay Velie
Albert, a groom	George Martin
Margaret, a maid	Mara Landi

Singers: Peggy Acheson, Marilynn Bradley, Deedy Irwin, Jane Johnston, Jean Kraemer, Mara Landi, Betty McGuire, Estelle Parsons, Noella Peloquin, Ginny Perlowin, Mary Roche, Kelley Stephens, Helene Whitney, Delbert Anderson, Edward Becker, Warren J. Brown, David Collyer, John Craig, Jack Dabdoub, Clifford Fearl, Robert C. Held, Carl Nicholas, Seth Riggs, Charles Rule, Mark Zeller

Dancers: Betty Carr, Alice Clift, Jane Fischer, Roberta Keith, Svetlana McLee, Patti Nestor, Wendy Nickerson, Fleur Rapp, Sigyn, Bob Bakanic, John Harmon, Jim Hutchison, Dick Korthaze, Eugene Louis, George Martin, Jim Moore, Lowell Purvis, Don Weissmuller, Roy Wilson

The Play's History

Happy Hunting opened on 6 December 1956 at the Majestic Theatre, New York, NY, and ran for 412 performances.

Synopsis

Liz Livingstone, an extremely ambitious socialite, resents not receiving an invitation to the wedding of Grace Kelly and Prince Rainier of Monaco, so she decides to stage an even more glittering affair by marrying her daughter to the Duke of Granada. What Livingstone could not predict was that she herself would fall in love with Granada, but the dramatic tension produced by that turn of events is soon released when Livingstone's daughter is actually in love with a lawyer, Sanford Stewart, Jr.

Commentary

Merman's personal popularity was about all that saved this "jerry-built and shopworn" show, which was characterized by clashes with Fernando Lamas and acrid litigation with an actor who claimed that Merman got him dismissed because he had dyed his hair gray to test for a part in another production. After the opening, the song "I'm Old Enough to Know Better" replaced "This Is What I Call Love," which appears on the original cast album. Two *Playbills*, one with a smiling, the other with a serious Merman on its cover, were distributed. Despite its problems, *Happy Hunting* returned $3,200,000 on a $500,000 investment.

Reviews: See **B28, B35, B45, B104, B174, B224, B230, B441, B473, B476, B522, B562, B588.**

S36   *GYPSY* (1959)

Credits

Book	Arthur Laurents
Music	Jule Styne
Lyrics	Stephen Sondheim
Producers	David Merrick, Leland Hayward
Director	Jerome Robbins
Musical Director	Milton Rosenstock
Choreographer	Jerome Robbins
Scenery Designer	Jo Mielziner
Costume Designer	Raoul Pene Du Bois

Cast

Uncle Jocko	Mort Marshall
George	Willie Sumner
Arnold	John Borden
Balloon Girl	Jody Lane
Baby Louise	Karen Moore
Rose	**Ethel Merman**
Baby June	Jacqueline Mayro
Newsboys	Bobby Brownell, Gene Castle, Steve Curry, Billy Harris
Pop	Erv Harmon
Weber	Joe Silver
Herbie	Jack Klugman
Louise	Sandra Church
June	Lane Bradbury
Tulsa	Paul Wallace
Yonkers	David Winters
Angie	Ian Tucker
L. A.	Michael Parks
Kringelein	Loney Lewis
Mr. Goldstone	Mort Marshall
Farm Boys	Marvin Arnold, Ricky Coll, Don Emmons, Ian Tucker, Michael

	Parks, Paul Wallace, David Winters
Miss Cratchitt	Peg Murray
Hollywood Blondes	
Agnes	Marilyn Cooper
Marjorie May	Patsy Bruder
Dolores	Marilyn D'Honau
Thelma	Merle Letowt
Edna	Joan Petlack
Gail	Imelda de Martin
Pastey	Richard Porter
Tessie Tura	Maria Karnilova
Mazeppa	Faith Dane
Cigar	Loney Lewis
Electra	Chotzi Foley
Showgirls	Kathryn Albertson, Gloria Kristy, Denise McLaglen, Barbara London, Theda Nelson, Carroll Jo Towers, Marie Wallace
Maid	Marsha Rivers
Phil	Joe Silver
Bougeron-Cochon	George Zima
Cow	Willie Sumner, George Zima

The Play's History

Gypsy opened on 21 May 1959 at the Broadway Theatre, New York, NY, and ran for 702 performances.

Warner Brothers released its film of the musical (with Rosalind Russell) in 1962.

Angela Lansbury starred in a London production that opened on 29 May 1973 at the Piccadilly Theatre.

The play was revived in New York in 1989 with Tyne Daly in Merman's role.

Synopsis

Rose, the awful epitome of the stage mother, is discovered rehearsing her children June and Louise for a second-rate children's show, but her ambition propels them against all opposition toward the big time. The name of the act changes as the years roll by, but

Rose's doggedness to make a star of the pretty
June leaves the plain Louise feeling inadequate. Rose's dreams are dashed when June
elopes with a dancer, but she recovers by de-
termining to make a star of Louise, a full-
time job that prevents her marrying her manag-
er Herbie. Eventually even Rose sees that
vaudeville is dying, but not before she discovers that Louise has made her debut as a
stripper after having been coached secretly.
Louise becomes a star, but not as Rose had
imagined. They quarrel bitterly, and Rose in
a devastating parody of Louise's act details
her frustrations and broken dreams. A recon-
ciliation of sorts with Louise occurs, and now
that her daughter has taken charge of her own
life, Rose, with Herbie's help, starts to
reassemble the pieces of hers.

Commentary

Merman received a telephone call from
Arthur Laurents, who was considering a
dramatic adaptation of Gypsy Rose Lee's
memoirs. He said, "I want to do a show. But I
don't want to do the usual Ethel Merman musical." Her response: "Neither do I. I want to
act." Laurents queried, "How far are you wil-
ling to go?" "As far as you want me to. Nobody's ever given me the chance before (**B307**,
p. 202)." It was a fortuitous interchange, because Mama Rose was, in Merman's estimation,
"the pinnacle of [her] career."

Reviews: See B17, B27, B69, B76, B85, B89,
B119, B209, B210, B211, B212, B213, B250,
B265, B270, B301, B333, B351, B440, B475,
B523, B539, B540, B565.

S37   *The Ethel Merman Show* (Las Vegas;
         Flamingo; 25 October 1962)

S38   *The Ethel Merman Show* (Summer 1963)

Merman and a group of entertainers appeared in numerous tents and outdoor theatres.

S39   *The Ethel Merman Show* (New York; Persian Room, Plaza Hotel; November 1963)

Review: See **B472**.

S40   *The Ethel Merman Show* (London; Talk of the Town; February 1964)

Reviews: See **B236, B312**.

S41   *The Ethel Merman Show* (Sydney, Australia; Sheraton Hotel; 1965)

S42   *ANNIE GET YOUR GUN*   (1966)

CREDITS

Book	Herbert and Dorothy Fields
Songs	Irving Berlin
Producer	Music Theatre of Lincoln Center
Director	Jack Sydow
Musical Director	Jonathan Anderson
Choreographer	Danny Daniels
Scenery Designer	Paul McGuire
Costume Designer	Frank Thompson

Cast

Little Boy	Jeffrey Scott
Little Girl	Deanna Melody
Charlie Davenport	Jerry Orbach
Dolly Tate	Benay Venuta
Iron Tail	Brynar Mehl
Yellow Foot	Gary Jendell
Mac	John Dorrin
Foster Wilson	Ronn Carroll
Frank Butler	Bruce Yarnell
The Shy Girl	Diana Banks
Annie Oakley	**Ethel Merman**
Little Jake	David Manning

Jessie	Jeanne Tanzy
Minnie	Holly Sherwood
Buffalo Bill	Rufus Smith
Mrs. Little Horse	Mary Falconer
Mrs. Black Tooth	Jaclynn Villamil
Mrs. Yellow Foot	Kuniko Narai
Indian Boy	Jeffrey Scott
Conductor	Jim Lynn
Porter	Beno Foster
Waiter	David Forssen
Pawnee Bill	Jack Dabdoub
Chief Sitting Bull	Harry Bellaver
The Wild Horse	Jaime Rogers
Pawnee's Messenger	Walt Hunter
Major Domo	Ben Laney
Mr. Schuyler Adams	Ronn Carroll
Mrs. Schuyler Adams	Patricia Hall
Dr. Ferguson	Marc Rowan
Mrs. Ferguson	Bobbi Baird
Mr. T. L. C. Keefer	Walt Hunter
Mr. Ernest Henderson	Grant Spalding
Mrs. Ernest Henderson	Lynn Carroll
Mrs. Sylvia Potter-Porter	Mary Falconer
Mr. Clay	John Dorrin

Singers: Bobbi Baird, Vicki Belmonte, Chrysten Carroll, Lynn Carroll, Audrey Dearden, Lynn Dovel, Mary Falconer, Patricia Hall, Florence Mercer, Susan Terry, Kenny Adams, Ronn Carroll, John Dorrin, David Forssen, Beno Foster, Walt Hunter, Ben Laney, Jim Lynn, Marc Rowan, Grant Spalding

Dancers: Diana Banks, Joanne Di Vito, Rozann Ford, Barbara Hancock, Ruth Lawrence, Kuniko Narai, Eva Marie Sage, Evelyn Taylor, Jaclynn Villamil, Anne Wallace, Bjarne Buchrup, Tony Catanzaro, Frank Derbas, Ronn Forella, Marcelo Gamboa, Jeremy Ives, Gary Jendell, Daniel Joel, Brynar Mehl, Gene Myers

The Play's History

Annie Get Your Gun opened on 31 May 1966 at the New York State Theatre, Lincoln Center for the Performing Arts, New York, NY, toured for a short time, and reopened at the Broadway Theatre and ran for 78 performances.

Synopsis: See **S30**.

Commentary

Undaunted by the possibility of unfavorable comparisons with her triumph of twenty years earlier, Merman tackled her old role with verve and a mature characterization. Her voice was better than ever, and with a much younger Frank Butler, she stopped every performance with Berlin's new counterpoint song, "Old-Fashioned Wedding."

Reviews: See **B36, B86, B269, B293, B417, B471, B474, B570.**

S43   *CALL ME MADAM* (St. Louis, MO; July 1968)

Merman performed with the St. Louis Municipal Opera.

S44   *CALL ME MADAM* (Kansas City, MO; 1969)

S45   *HELLO, DOLLY!* (1970)

Credits

Book	Michael Stewart
Songs	Jerry Herman
Producer	David Merrick
Director	Gower Champion, Lucia Victor
Musical Director	Saul Schechtman
Choreographer	Gower Champion, Lucia Victor
Scenery Designer	Oliver Smith
Costume Designer	Freddy Wittop

Cast

Mrs. Dolly Gallagher Levi	**Ethel Merman**
Ernestina	Marcia Lewis
Ambrose Kemper	David Gary
Horse Patty Pappathatos,	Ellen Elias
Horace Vandergelder	Jack Goode
Ermengarde	Patricia Cope
Cornelius Hackl	Russell Nype
Barnaby Tucker	Danny Lockin
Irene Malloy	June Helmers
Minnie Fay	Georgia Engel
Mrs. Rose	Joyce Dahl
Rudolph	James Beard
Judge	George Blackwell
Court Clerk	Dick Crowley

Townspeople, waiters, etc.: Beverly Baker, Maggie Benson, Monica Carter, Joyce Dahl, Ellen Elias, Gwen Hillier, Lee Hooper, Irma Kingsley, Janice Painchaud, Patty Pappathatos, Jacqueline Payne, Pat Trott, Elise Warner, Paul Berne, George Blackwell, Ted Bloecher, Wayne Bond, Jack Craig, Ron Crofoot, Dick Crowley, Richard Dodd, Mark East, David Evans, Ed Goldsmid, Joseph Helms, Jim Hovis, Robert L. Jultman, J. David Kirby, Sean Nolan

The Play's History

Hello, Dolly! opened on 16 January 1964 at the St. James Theatre, New York, NY, and ran for 2,844 performances. Ethel Merman assumed the role of Dolly on 28 March 1970.

Mary Martin played Dolly on tour in the U. S., the Far East, and London, opening there at Drury Lane on 2 December 1965. Martin was replaced by Dora Bryan, who led the cast to 794 performances.

The musical was filmed in 1969 with Barbra Streisand in the leading role.

Synopsis

The play opens in Yonkers, NY, in 1898, where matchmaker Dolly Levi, widow of a dry-goods merchant, is busy trying to find a marriage partner for Horace Vandergelder, also a merchant. Although Dolly sees herself as the second Mrs. Vandergelder, the gentleman himself is enamored of a New York milliner, one Irene Molloy. When Vandergelder goes to New York to meet Mrs. Molloy, his two clerks Cornelius and Barnaby close the shop and head for the big city as well. At the millinery shop they meet Irene and her assistant Minnie Fay, and when Vandergelder suddenly appears, they must hide from him. Vandergelder eventually discovers that his "intended" is hiding men in her shop, so he decides to have nothing more to do with her. Dolly discovers what has happened and arranges for Cornelius and Barnaby to escort Irene and Minnie Fay to the elegant Harmonia Gardens, where later Dolly herself makes a spectacular entry. Dolly meets Vandergelder at the restaurant and does everything she can to interest him in her. She is not entirely unsuccessful, but Vandergelder sees his clerks, fires Cornelius and Barnaby, and behaves so boisterously that he is taken to jail. Later he realizes that he is without shop help and probably without Dolly. When his despair is greatest, Dolly appears, hears his proposal, and agrees to marry him.

Commentary

The role of Dolly was written with Merman in mind. When she declined to commit herself to another potentially long run, the part was altered to fit Carol Channing. Five subsequent actresses propelled the production toward becoming Broadway's longest-running musical. With that achievement in view, David Merrick persuaded Merman to be Broadway's seventh and last Dolly. Jerry Herman restored two songs that had been omitted because they were uniquely suited to Merman: "World, Take Me Back" and "Love, Look in My Window." Since both are critical to the plot, particularly to the development of Dolly's character, the version in which Merman appeared was considerably enhanced.

Reviews: See **B165**, **B186**, **B252**.

S46   *The Ethel Merman Show* (London; Palladium Theatre; 9 September 1974)

Reviews: See **B303**, **B535**.

S47   *Salute to Joshua Logan* (New York; 2 May 1975)

This performance was in aid of the Museum of the City of New York.

S48   *Ethel Merman in Concert with the Boston Pops Orchestra* (Boston; Symphony Hall; May 1975)

This show was taped and aired on 4 July 1976.

S49   *Ethel Merman in Concert with the Nashville Symphony Orchestra* (Nashville, TN; Grand Ole Opry House; 16 September 1976)

Review: See **B591**.

S50   *Ethel Merman in Concert with the Wichita Symphony Orchestra* (Wichita, KS; 16 March 1977)

S51   *Together on Broadway* (New York; 15 May 1977)

This concert, in aid of the Museum of the City of New York, reunited Merman and Mary Martin.

Reviews: See **B192, B450**.

S52   *Ethel Merman in Concert with the Seattle Symphony* (Seattle, WA; Opera House; 6 June 1977)

S53   *Ethel Merman in Concert with the Dallas Symphony Orchestra* (Dallas, TX; Summertop Tent at Worth Park; 10 June 1977)

S54   *Ethel Merman in Concert with the Chatauqua Symphony Orchestra* (Chatauqua, NY; Amphitheatre; 14 July 1977)

S55   *Ethel Merman in Concert with the Denver Symphony Orchestra* (Denver, CO; Red Rock Amphitheatre; 22 July 1977)

S56   *Ethel Merman in Concert with the Los Angeles Philharmonic Orchestra* (Los Angeles, CA; Hollywood Bowl; 2 August 1977)

Reviews: See **B315, B465**.

S57   *Ethel Merman in Concert with the Minnesota Orchestra* (Minneapolis, MN; Orchestra Hall; 23 & 24 July 1977)

S58   *Ethel Merman in Concert* (West Point, NY; United States Military Academy; 8 October 1977)

S59   *Ethel Merman in Concert* (Oklahoma City, OK; Civic Center; 12 November 1977)

S60   *Ethel Merman in Concert* (Orlando, FL; Atlantis Theatre; 20 November 1977)

S61   *Ethel Merman in Concert with the Indianapolis Symphony Orchestra* (Indianapolis, IN; Clowes Hall; 29 January 1978)

S62   *Ethel Merman in Concert with the Detroit Symphony Orchestra* (Detroit, MI; Ford Hall; 3 & 5 February 1978)

S63   *Ethel Merman in Concert with the Norfolk Symphony Orchestra* (Norfolk, VA; Chrysler Hall; 18 April 1978)

S64   *Ethel Merman in Concert with the Kansas City Philharmonic Orchestra* (Kansas City, MO; Music Hall; 11 February 1978)

S65   *Ethel Merman in Concert* (Richmond, VA; William and Mary Hall; 14 February 1978)

S66   *Ethel Merman in Concert* (Pittsburgh, PA; Heinz Hall; 14 & 15 July 1978)

S67   *Ethel Merman in Concert* (Philadelphia, PA; Robin Hood Dell West; 27 July 1978)

S68   *Ethel Merman in Concert with the Los Angeles Philharmonic Orchestra* (Los Angeles, CA; Hollywood Bowl; 11 & 12 August 1978)

Reviews: See **B120, B363**.

S69   *Ethel Merman in Concert with the Rochester Philharmonic Orchestra* (Rochester, NY; Highland Bowl; 1 & 2 September 1978)

S70   *Ethel Merman in Concert with the Minnesota Orchestra* (Minneapolis, MN; Orchestra Hall; 16 & 17 September 1978)

S71   *Ethel Merman in Concert* (Rockford, IL; Coronado Theatre; 28 September 1978)

S72   *Ethel Merman in Concert* (Providence, RI; Ocean State Performing Arts Center; 6 October 1978)

S73   *Ethel Merman in Concert with the Hamilton Philharmonic Orchestra* (Hamilton, Ont., 24 & 25 November 1978)

S74   *Ethel Merman in Concert* (Buffalo, NY; Convention Hall; 3 February 1979)

S75   *Ethel Merman in Concert with the North Carolina Symphony Orchestra* (Raleigh, NC; Memorial Auditorium; 13 & 14 March 1979)

S76   *Ethel Merman in Concert with the Springfield Symphony Orchestra* (Springfield, MA; Civic Center; 30 March 1979)

S77   *Ethel Merman in Concert with the Milwaukee Symphony Orchestra* (Milwaukee, WI; Milwaukee Auditorium; 9 June 1979)

S78   *Ethel Merman in Concert with the Atlanta Symphony Orchestra* (Atlanta, GA; 20 & 22 June 1979)

S79   *Ethel Merman in Concert with the Baltimore Symphony Orchestra* (Baltimore, MD; Merriweather Post Pavilion; 8 July 1979)

S80   *Ethel Merman in Concert* (Rochester, MI; Meadow Brook Theatre at Oakland University; 15 July 1979)

S81   *Ethel Merman in Concert with the South Dakota Symphony Orchestra* (Brookings, SD; Open Air Theatre at South Dakota State University; 20, 21, & 22 July 1979)

S82   *Ethel Merman in Concert* (Saratoga, NY; Performing Arts Center; 11 August 1979)

S83   *Ethel Merman in Concert with the Syracuse Symphony Orchestra* (Syracuse, NY; Civic Center; 12 September 1979)

S84   *Ethel Merman in Concert with the Springfield Symphony Orchestra* (Springfield, MA; Civic Center; 4 November 1979)

S85   *Ethel Merman in Concert* (Canton, OH; Memorial Civic Center; 30 April 1980)

S86   *Ethel Merman in Concert with the Richmond Symphony* (Richmond, VA; The Mosque; 3 May 1980)

Reviews: See **B63**, **B66**.

S87   *Ethel Merman in Concert* (Seattle, WA; Fifth Avenue Theatre; 16 June 1980)

S88   *Ethel Merman in Concert* (Hempstead, NY; Calderone Theatre; 14-15 March 1981)

S89   *Ethel Merman in Concert with the Roanoke Symphony Orchestra* (Roanoke, VA, 9 May 1981)

S90   *Ethel Merman in Concert with the Philadelphia Orchestra* (Philadelphia, PA; Mann Music Center; 18 June 1981)

S91   *Ethel Merman in Concert at Carnegie Hall* (New York; 3 May 1982)

Reviews: See **B32, B91, B319, B576.**

S92   *Ethel Merman in Concert* (New Orleans, LA; Municipal Auditorium; 2 & 3 July 1982)

S93   *Royal Command Variety Performance* (London; Theatre Royal, Drury Lane; 8 November 1982)

In the presence of H. M. Queen Elizabeth, the Queen Mother, and other members of the royal family, Merman sang "There's No Business Like Show Business" in the finale of a show on the theme of timeless musicals.

Review: See **B457.**

Radio and Television Appearances

R01   *The Louis Calhern Show* (1930?)

Merman sang a medley of songs from *Girl Crazy*.

R02   *The Gus Van Show* (4 January 1931; ABC; 15 minutes)

Merman appeared as a guest on this show, but she did not sing.

Review: See **B425**.

R03   *Carnegie Hall* (1934)

Vinton Freedley introduced Merman and William Gaxton, who joined her in "You're the Top" after she sang "I Get a Kick out of You."

R04   *Rhythm at 8* (1935; CBS)

Merman's twelve weeks as hostess of this musical variety show under the musical direction of Al Goodman ended when contractual obligations required her presence in Hollywood.

Reviews: See **B426**, **B446**.

R05   *Gershwin Memorial* (13 July 1937; WHN)

"I Got Rhythm" was Merman's tribute to the deceased composer.

R06   *The Jimmy Durante Show* (1939)

Merman sang "It's All Yours."

R07   *Keep 'Em Rolling* (9 November 1941; Sun Mutual; 30 minutes)

Merman recorded the theme song (Rodgers and Hart's "The Flame of Freedom Is Burning") of this radio program that was sponsored by the Office of Emergency Management. Arthur Kurlan produced, and Morton Gould was the musical director.

Review: See **B428**.

R08   *The Chamber Music Society of Lower Basin Street* (1944; NBC: Blue Network)

After talking about her new show, *Sadie Thompson*, and trading repartee with Johnny Johnston, Merman sang "The Very Thought of You."

R09   *Stagedoor Canteen* (12 January 1945; ABC)

Merman appeared with William Gaxton on this show that featured Bert Lytell as emcee. Music was provided by Raymond Paige, and Earle McGill directed.

R10   *Philco Radio Time: The Bing Crosby Show* (11 June 1947; NBC; 30 minutes)

R11   *Philco Radio Time: The Bing Crosby Show* (11 May 1948; NBC; 30 minutes)

Of this appearance, Merman wrote, "Radio was so relaxing. I decided it interested me (**B307**, p. 152)."

T01   *Texaco Star Theatre: The Milton Berle Show* (22 March 1948; NBC)

Although a reviewer thought this was Merman's TV debut, it might have been her second program with Berle. She sang a medley of "Smile, Darn You, Smile," "Smiles," and "When You're Smiling." Berle joined her in "You're the Top."

Review: See **B504**.

R12   *Philco Radio Time: The Bing Crosby Show* (23 March 1949; NBC; 30 minutes)

R13   *The Ford Show* (20 June 1949)

In a clear attempt to imitate the Mary Martin/Ezio Pinza team, Merman was presented with operatic tenor Lauritz Melchior with whom she sang "Anything You Can Do, I Can Do Better." "There's No Business Like Show Business" was her solo.

Review: See **B505**.

T02   *Thru the Crystal Ball* (20 June 1949; CBS; 30 minutes)

Jimmy Savo was the original host of this show that dramatized fables in dance form. When he left, Merman was a guest hostess on this one program.

R14   *The Ethel Merman Show* (31 July 1949; NBC)

The cast included Leon Janney and Allan Drake in a show about the difficulty of assembling a revue, thus allowing the cast to try out various songs and bits. Will Glickman and Joe Stein wrote the scripts, which were directed by Kenneth MacGregor.

Reviews: See **B245**, **B311**, **B420**.

R15   *Philco Radio Time: The Bing Crosby Show* (22 March 1950; NBC; 30 minutes)

R16   *The Big Show* (5 November 1950; NBC; 90 minutes)

Produced and directed by Dee Engelbach, the show featured Tallulah Bankhead as hostess. Among the guests on this inaugural broadcast were Jimmy Durante, Fred Allen and Portland Hoffa, Danny Thomas, and Jose Ferrer. Merman, Paul Lukas, and Russell Nype devoted eight minutes to songs from *Call Me Madam*, and Merman traded insults with Bankhead.

Review: See **B429**.

R17   *The Big Show* (4 March 1951; NBC; 90 minutes)

Merman and Margaret Truman were the principal guests.

Review: See **B421**.

R18   *The Big Show* (29 April 1951; NBC; 90 minutes)

Merman quipped with hostess Tallulah Bankhead and sang "There's No Business Like Show Business." Milton Berle was also a guest.

Review: See **B430**.

R19   *The Big Show* (14 October 1951; NBC; 90 minutes)

Merman sang "Alexander's Ragtime Band" and "Over the Rainbow." Then "Love Is the Reason" was rendered by a sextette including Merman, Tallulah Bankhead, Shirley Booth, Jimmy Durante, Fred Allen, and George Sanders.

Review: See **B422**.

R20   *The Jack Benny Salute* (9 November 1951; CBS; 30 minutes)

Benny's friends honored him on the radio at the very moment he was being "roasted" at the Friars' Club. Merman, Milton Berle, and Ronald and Benita Colman appeared, Merman singing "There's No Business Like Show Business."

Review: See **B431**.

R21   *The Big Show* (3 February 1952; NBC; 90 minutes)

Although Vera Lynn and Cathleen Nesbitt were guests, Merman dominated the show with her acid interchanges with Tallulah Bankhead and her rendition of "Zing Went the Strings of My Heart" and "It's a Great, Big Wonderful World."

Review: See **B423**.

R22   *The Big Show* (9 March 1952; NBC; 90 minutes)

R23   *The Big Show* (20 April 1952; NBC; 90 minutes)

Fred Allen and Groucho Marx were guests. Merman's solo was "Heat Wave" and her duet (with George Sanders) "Marrying for Love."

Review: See **B424**.

T03   *Ed Sullivan's Toast of the Town* (29 March 1953; CBS; 60 minutes)

T04   *The Ford 50th Anniversary Show* (15 June 1953; CBS and NBC; 120 minutes)

Produced by Leland Hayward. Directed by Clark Jones. See *Discography* (**D30**) for a complete list of the songs that comprised Merman and Martin's twelve-minute duet. Over 200 copies of the recording were sold in the first ten days of release. Ethen Mordden observed of this show, "It was perhaps the last time that the country turned as a unit to the Broadway musical (**B322**, p. 114)."

Cast

Ethel Merman   Rudy Vallee
Mary Martin   Eddie Fisher
Edward R. Murrow   Teddy Wilson
Marian Anderson   Howard Lindsay
Kukla, Fran, and Ollie   Dorothy Stickney
Wally Cox   Bill Lawrence

Review: See **B454**.

T05   *Dinner with the President* (1953)

T06   *Colgate Comedy Hour: The Ethel Merman Show* (24 January 1954; NBC; 60 minutes)

In addition to Merman as hostess, Jimmy Durante and Gene Nelson were guests. Her first number was "Just a Lady with a Song," followed by "Love Is Sweeping the Country," "I Love Paris," and "C'est Magnifique." Merman was justifiably indignant that her rendition of "I Got Rhythm" was accompanied by breaking glass, falling pictures, and other similar sight gags. On the show she received the Hollywood Correspondents' Award for her work in *Call Me Madam*. The producer/director was Joseph Santley, and the writers, Charles Isaacs and Jackie Elinson.

T07   *Colgate Comedy Hour: Anything Goes* (28 February 1954; NBC; 60 minutes)

Ethel Merman, Frank Sinatra, and Bert Lahr starred in this tabloid version of Merman's hit show of 1934. Book by Guy Bolton and P. G. Wodehouse, revised by Howard Lindsay and Russel Crouse. Music and lyrics by Cole Porter. Musical direction by Al Goodman. See *Discography* (**D34**) for a complete list of musical numbers. Sinatra's numbers, although written by Cole Porter, were interpolated, as was Lahr's duet with Merman of "Friendship," from *Du Barry Was a Lady*.

Cast

Reno Sweeney	**Ethel Merman**
Billy Crocker	Frank Sinatra
Reverend Dr. Moon	Bert Lahr
Bonnie	Sheree North

Reviews: See **B14**, **B196**.

T08   *Best of Broadway: Panama Hattie* (10 November 1954; CBS; 60 minutes)

Merman was assisted by Ray Middleton, Art Carney, and Jack E. Leonard in this adaptation of her hit show of 1940. Book by Herbert Fields and B. G. De Sylva. Music and lyrics by Cole Porter. See *Discography* (**D35**) for a complete list of musical numbers.

Cast

Hattie Maloney	**Ethel Merman**
Nick Bullett	Ray Middleton
Woozy	Art Carney
Windy	Jack E. Leonard
Charlie Randolph	Neil Hamilton

Review: See **B192**.

R24   *Suspense: Never Follow a Banjo Act*
             (1954?; CBS; 60 minutes)

Merman acted a straight role in this drama.

T09   *Shower of Stars: The Show Stoppers*
             (20 January 1955; CBS; 60 minutes)

Red Skelton, Bobby Van, and the Kean Sisters were Merman's co-stars and David Rose the musical director. Jule Styne and Nat Perrin produced, and Seymour Berns directed. James Starbuck won an Emmy for Best Choreographer. In the first part Merman rendered "A Little Girl from Little Rock" and in the second, "Papa, Won't You Dance with Me?". Her other numbers included "Eadie Was a Lady," "There's No Business Like Show Business," and "You're Just in Love" (with Skelton).

Review: See **B533**.

T10   *Shower of Stars: Ethel Merman's Show Stoppers* (14 April 1955; CBS; 60 minutes)

Merman was assisted by Red Skelton, Peter Lind Hayes, Mary Healey, Harold Lang, and Andy Robinson. She sang "I Got Rhythm," and "All of You." The production staff was the same as for **T09**.

Reviews: See **B469**, **B534**.

T11   *Ed Sullivan's Toast of the Town* (17 July 1955; CBS; 60 minutes)

"The Hostess with the Mostes' on the Ball" was Merman's solo. In the finale she sang "That's the Kind of Dame I Am." Russell

Nype joined her for "You're Just in Love."

Review: See **B510**.

T12   *Person to Person* (9 September 1955;
             CBS; 30 minutes)

Edward R. Murrow interviewed Merman in her home in Denver, CO.

T13   *The Chevy Show* (6 December 1955;
             CBS)

Merman was a guest artist on this variety show with Bob Cummings as host. Other guests were Tennessee Ernie Ford, Jonathan Winters, and Shirley MacLaine. Merman sang a medley of "I Love a Piano," "The Lady Is a Tramp," "The Gypsy in My Soul," and state songs ("Oklahoma," "California Here I Come," etc. At the closing she sang "Friendship" with Tennessee Ernie.

Reviews: See **B418**, **B506**.

T14   *The Music of Gershwin* (1955)

Merman joined Cab Calloway, Alfred Drake, and Tony Bennett in this tribute to her friend and mentor.

T15   *G. E. Theater: Reflected Glory* (25
             March 1956; CBS; 30 minutes)

Even Merman claimed to be dissatisfied with her performance in a straight dramatic role in this adaptation of George Kelly's play.

Review: See **B468**.

T16   *U. S. Steel Hour: Honest in the Rain*
             (9 May 1956; CBS; 60 minutes)

Merman's non-singing role in this drama was that of "a lonely horseplayer."

Review: See **B468**.

T17   *Masquerade Party* (1956; ABC; 30 minutes)

In this game show, panelists tried to guess the identities of heavily disguised guests, one of whom was Merman made up as a gas station attendant--a pun on ethyl gas.

T18   *The Perry Como Show* (December 1957; CBS; 60 minutes)

Merman and Como sang "When the Red, Red Robin Comes Bob, Bob, Bobbin' Along." She virtually stopped the show with "Waiting for the Robert E. Lee," "You Made Me Love You," and "Alexander's Ragtime Band." The choice of songs suggests the theme of a tribute to Al Jolson.

Review: See **B507**.

T19   *The Eddie Fisher Show* (1958?; NBC; 60 minutes)

Merman chatted with Fisher about her role in *Gypsy* and joined him in a duet of "you" songs.

T20   *The Dinah Shore Show* (1958?; NBC; 60 minutes)

T21   *The Frank Sinatra Show* (25 April 1958; ABC; 30 minutes)

Merman sang "Zing Went the Strings of My Heart" and "That Old Feeling" before joining Sinatra in a duet of "You're the Top."

T22   *The Perry Como Show* (November 1958; CBS; 60 minutes)

T23   *The Ed Sullivan Show* (11 October 1959; CBS; 60 minutes)

Merman sang "There'll Be Some Changes Made" and "I'm Glad There Is You."

Review: See **B537**.

T24   *Ford Startime: Merman on Broadway* (24 November 1959; NBC; 60 minutes)

The producer of record was Hubbell Robinson, but Roger Edens played a pivotal role in providing Merman's material. Tab Hunter, Tom Poston, and Fess Parker also appeared.

Reviews: See **B97, B197**.

T25   *The Bell Telephone Hour: The Four of Us* (1960; NBC; 60 minutes)

Beatrice Lillie, Ray Bolger, and Benny Goodman joined Merman in a ragtime medley. Merman's solo was "I Got Rhythm."

T26   *The Gershwin Years* (15 January 1961; CBS; 90 minutes)

In addition to Merman, the cast included Maurice Chevalier, Frank Sinatra, Florence Henderson, and Julie London. Merman's songs were "Strike up the Band," "Embraceable You," "Somebody Loves Me," and "I Got Rhythm." With Sinatra she sang "Let's Call the Whole Thing Off." Leland Hayward and Marshall Jamison produced, and Norman Campbell directed.

Reviews: See **B280, B453**.

T27   *An Evening with Ethel Merman* (9 May 1961; BBC)

Merman's popular cabaret act at the Talk of the Town was filmed live and televised on British TV, but the American networks chose not to broadcast the program.

T28   *The Academy Awards Show* (April 1962)

Merman performed a medley of songs by Irving Berlin.

T29   *The Bob Hope Show* (20 November 1962; NBC; 60 minutes)

Merman performed a medley of "smile" songs and a sketch set in Tokyo with Hope.

T30   *The Perry Como Show* (18 January 1963; NBC; 60 minutes)

T31   *Lincoln Center Day* (22 September 1963; CBS; 60 minutes)

Merman joined a bevy of musical performers in this celebration of the opening of Lincoln Center, but she was the only one accorded a spectacular entrance by rising magically out of the orchestra pit. The show was produced by Robert Saudek and directed by Norman Abbott.

Review: See **B206**.

T32   *Maggie Brown* (23 September 1963; CBS; 30 minutes)

The pilot of a situation comedy starring Merman, *Maggie Brown* was unsuccessful. The supporting cast included Susan Watson, with whom Merman sang "Mutual Admiration Society" and "Friendship."

T33   *The Judy Garland Show: Tea for Two* (6 October 1963; CBS; 60 minutes)

Merman, supposedly discovered in the audience, sang a few bars of "You're Just in Love" before joining Garland and guest Barbra Streisand for "tea" on stage. After a few moments' chatter, the three sang "There's No Business Like Show Business."

Review: See **B508**.

R25   *The Helen Hall Show* (November 1963)

T34   *The Judy Garland Show* (12 January 1964; CBS; 60 minutes)

Merman joined Garland, Shelley Berman, Peter Gennaro, and Dancers for a medley: "Ev'rybody's Doin' It"/"Let's Do It." Merman later sang "Gee! But It's Good to Be Here." She taped "That Old Feeling," but it was deleted. Then she delivered the almost obligatory "I Get a Kick out of You." Late in the show came the Merman-Garland medley: "Friendship"/"Let's Be Buddies"/"You're the Top"/ "You're Just in Love"/"It's De-Lovely"/ "Together (Wherever We Go)"

T35   *Bell Telephone Hour: Tribute to Cole Porter* (28 January 1964; NBC; 60 minutes)

Donald Vorhees was the musical director. Merman's opening medley included "Another Opening, Another Show," "It's De-Lovely," "Anything Goes," "From This Moment On," "Ridin' High," and "We Open in Venice." Later she sang a medley of "Easy to Love," "You'd Be So Nice to Come Home To," "What Is This Thing Called Love?," "You Do Something to Me," "I Get a Kick out of You," "Blow, Gabriel, Blow," "Down in the Depths on the 90th Floor," "Let's Be Buddies," "Friendship," and "You're the Top." Merman also served as hostess.

Review: See **B509**.

T36   *The Lucy Show: Lucy Teaches Ethel Merman to Sing* (1 June 1964; CBS; 30 minutes)

T37   *The Red Skelton Show* (1964?; CBS; 60 minutes)

T38   *The Hollywood Palace with Fred Astaire* (1965; ABC; 60 minutes)

The executive producer was Nick Vanoff, and the musical director was Mitchell Ayres. Merman's solo was "Some People." While teaching Astaire to sing loudly, the pair sang a duet.

T39   *Kraft Suspense Theater: 'Twixt the Cup and Lip* (3 June 1965; NBC; 60 minutes)

In addition to Merman, the cast included Larry Blyden, Jean Hale, Joan Blackman, Charles McGraw, Lane Bradford, John Hoyt, and Lee Patterson.

R26   *The Martha Dean Show* (22 October 1965)

Merman spoke enthusiastically about her recent trip to the Soviet Union with her son.

T40   *Gypsy Rose Lee and Friends* (1965; Syndicated; 90 minutes)

Lee and Merman chat while watching home movies of rehearsals of *Gypsy*.

T41   *The Ed Sullivan Shown* (13 February 1966; CBS; 60 minutes)

T42   *The Ed Sullivan Show* (25 September 1966; CBS; 60 minutes)

T43   *The Ed Sullivan Show* (8 January 1967; CBS; 60 minutes)

T44   *Annie Get Your Gun* (19 March 1967; NBC; 90 minutes)

This production was produced by Clark Jones and directed by Jones and Jack Sydow.

Reviews: See **B111**, **B195**.

T45   *That Girl: Pass the Potatoes, Ethel Merman* (7 September 1967; ABC; 30 minutes)

Marlo Thomas devoted nearly her whole show to Merman.

Review: See **B511**.

T46   *Batman: The Sport of Penguins* (5 October 1967; ABC; 30 minutes)

Merman's villainous character was called Lola Lasagna.

T47   *Batman: A Horse of Another Color* (12 October 1967; ABC; 30 minutes)

T48   *The Ed Sullivan Show* (15 October 1967; CBS; 60 minutes)

T49   *Tarzan: Mountains of the Moon* (24 November, 1 December 1967; NBC)

Merman played a singing missionary.

T50   *That Girl: The Other Woman* (1 February 1968; ABC; 30 minutes)

T51   *The Ed Sullivan Show* (5 May 1968; CBS; 90 minutes)

Merman appeared in celebration of Irving Berlin's 80th birthday.

Review: See **B538**.

T52   *Around the World of Mike Todd* (8 September 1968; ABC; 60 minutes)

Merman was featured because Todd produced *Something for the Boys*. Michael Todd, Jr. wrote and produced the TV show.

Review: See **B198**.

T53   *That's Life* (29 October 1968; ABC; 60 minutes)

Merman was the guest star in this musical comedy starring Robert Morse, E. J. Peaker, Shelley Berman, and Kay Medford. She sang "Think Pink" and other songs.

T54   *The Mike Douglas Show* (30 January 1969; Syndicated; 90 minutes)

Merman was co-host of the week, and her grandchildren were featured guests.

T55   *The Carol Burnett Show* (3 March 1969; CBS; 60 minutes)

In addition to a duet with Burnett, Merman sang "Gentle on My Mind."

T56   *The Tony Awards* (20 Apr. 1969; NBC; 90 minutes)

Merman presented the award for the best direction to Peter Hunt of *1776*.

T57   *The Merv Griffin Show* (2 December 1969; CBS; 90 minutes)

T58   *The Merv Griffin Show* (13 August 1970; CBS; 90 minutes)

T59   *The Merv Griffin Show* (29 April 1971; CBS; 90 minutes)

T60   *This Is Your Life* (20 May 1971; NBC; 30 minutes)

Merman was the subject of Ralph Edwards' tribute, which was rebroadcasted after her death.

T61   *Jack Lemmon in 'S Wonderful, 'S Marvelous, 'S Gershwin* (17 January 1972; NBC)

Merman's contribution was "I Got Rhythm."

Review: See **B346**.

T62   *The Tony Awards* (23 April 1972)

Merman received a special award for her contributions to the theatre. Assisted by Hal Linden and Larry Blyden, she sang "I Got Rhythm," "I Get a Kick out of You," "Make It Another Old-Fashioned, Please," "You Can't Get a Man with a Gun," and "Everything's Coming up Roses."

Review: See **B443**.

T63   *The Merv Griffin Show* (19 November 1972; Syndicated; 90 minutes)

T64   *Ed Sullivan's Broadway* (16 March 1973; CBS; 90 minutes)

The cast included Jack Cassidy, Julie Harris, Lou Jacobi, Michele Lee, Marilyn Michaels, Frank Sinatra, Jr., Melvin Van Peebles, Bobby Van, Gwen Verdon, and Cyril Ritchard. Merman performed "interesting reprises" of her stage successes as well as "When the Lights Go on Again" and a medley of songs from shows produced by Hal Prince.

Review: See **B343**.

T65   *The Tonight Show* (14 February 1975; NBC; 105 minutes)

T66   *Dinah* (26 February 1975; Syndicated; 90 and 60 minutes)

    Dinah Shore was the hostess of this talk show.

T67   *Dinah* (10 March 1975; Syndicated; 90 and 60 minutes)

T68   *The Tonight Show* (26 March 1975; NBC; 105 minutes)

T69   *The Tonight Show* (12 May 1975; NBC; 105 minutes)

T70   *The Mike Douglas Show* (12 May 1975; Syndicated; 90 minutes)

T71   *The Merv Griffin Show* (8 September 1975; Syndicated; 90 minutes)

T72   *Dinah* (31 January 1976; Syndicated; 90 and 60 minutes)

T73   *The Merv Griffin Show* (27 April 1976; Syndicated; 90 minutes)

T74   *Evening at the Pops* (4 July 1976; PBS; 60 minutes)

    Although this concert was filmed in 1975, it was saved to be shown as part of the U. S. Bicentennial celebration. Arthur Fiedler was the musical director.

T75   *Dinah* (9 July 1976; Syndicated; 90 and 60 minutes)

T76   *The Big Event: The Big Party* (27 September 1976; NBC; 90 minutes)

Merman appeared on the premiere broadcast of this omnibus program, the format of which changed weekly. She strode in the rain through Shubert Alley singing "Everything's Coming up Roses" and ended up at Sardi's where she was joined by Marvin Hamlisch at the piano. They performed "Sweet Georgia Brown," "What I Did for Love," "Get Me to the Church on Time," and "All That Jazz."

Review: See **B536**.

T77   *Entertainment Hall of Fame* (26 October 1976)

Nominating George Gershwin, Cole Porter, and Irving Berlin, Merman sang "I Got Rhythm," "I Get a Kick out of You," and "There's No Business Like Show Business."

T78   *Ted Knight Musical Comedy Variety Special* (30 November 1976; CBS; 60 minutes)

Merman's talents were added to those of Edward Asner, Fred MacMurray, Rue McClanahan, Phil Silvers, and Loretta Swit. Directed by Sid Smith. Musical director: Peter Matz.

Review: See **B345**.

T79   *Steve Lawrence-Edie Gormé From This Moment On. . . Cole Porter Special* (10 March 1977; ABC; 60 minutes)

Produced by Gary Smith and Dwight Hemion, who also directed, this tribute featured Merman and Bob Hope. Merman sang "I'm Throwing a

Ball Tonight," "Well, Did You Evah?," "Make It Another Old-Fashioned, Please," and others.

T80   *The Merv Griffin Show* (10 March 1977; Syndicated; 90 minutes)

In addition to Merman, Griffin's guests were Karen Morrow, Dolores Gray, and Ann Miller. The theme was "the belters."

T81   *Lifestyles with Beverly Sills* (29 March 1977)

Sills is joined both by Merman and Mary Martin, who were promoting *Together on Broadway*.

T82   *The Merv Griffin Show* (14 April 1977; Syndicated; 90 minutes))

Another show on the "belters" brought together Kaye Ballard, Bernadette Peters, Barbara Cook, and Merman. Merman performed "the medley."

T83   *The Today Show* (13 May 1977; NBC; 120 minutes)

Merman and Mary Martin talked of their forthcoming appearance in *Together on Broadway*.

T84   *You're Gonna Love It Here* (1 June 1977; CBS; 30 minutes)

In this unsold pilot for a situation comedy, Merman played "Dolly Rogers," a star of musical comedy. Her son was played by Austin Pendleton. The executive producer was Frank Konigsberg; the producer, Mel Farber; directors, Gordon Rigby and Bruce Paltrow; the music director, Peter Matz; and the writer, Bruce Paltrow.

T85   *The Merv Griffin Show* (15 May 1978; Syndicated; 90 minutes)

T86   *The Merv Griffin Show* (13 November 1978; Syndicated; 90 minutes)

Recorded on 22 October, this program featured Merman singing "All Alone" and "All by Myself."

T87   *Christmas Eve on Sesame Street* (3 December 1978; CTW)

Merman sings "Tomorrow" and a medley of Christmas songs.

T88   *Ford 75th Anniversary Show* (1978)

Merman sang "Before the Parade Passes By."

T89   *American Pop: The Great Singers* (10 January 1979; EBC-TV)

Merman's segment featured a collection of her memorable songs, "the Merman medley," with interspersed narration.

T90   *The Merv Griffin Show* (9 May 1979; Syndicated; 90 minutes)

T91   *The Love Boat: Third Wheel* (12 May 1979; ABC; 60 minutes)

Merman had a continuing role as "Rosie Smith," the mother of "Burl ('Gopher') Smith."

T92   *Musical Comedy Tonight* (1 October 1979; PBS; 90 minutes)

Produced by Sylvia Fine, this show displayed Merman in three songs from *Anything Goes* in which she wore replicas of her original costumes. With Rock Hudson she sang

"You're the Top." While taping this show, Merman experienced a couple of episodes of loss of memory.

Review: See **B512**.

T93   *The Merv Griffin Show* (5 October 1979; Syndicated; 90 minutes)

T94   *Rudolph and Frosty's Christmas in July* (ABC; 25 Nov. 1979; 97 minutes; Video: Vestron)

Credits

Directors   Arthur Rankin, Jr.,
                                              Jules Bass

Cast

Voices: Red Buttons, **Ethel Merman**, Mickey Rooney, Shelley Winters, Alan Sues, Jackie Vernon

Synopsis

Rudolph and Frosty "team up for a holiday celebration in summertime."

T95   *The Jack Jones Special*

When taping this show in Hamilton, Ontario, Merman fell and injured herself.

T96   *The Love Boat: Not So Fast Gopher* (9 February 1980; ABC)

Merman appeared again as "Rosie Smith."

T97   *The Merv Griffin Show* (24 April 1980; Syndicated; 90 minutes)

T98   *The Merv Griffin Show* (22 September 1980; Syndicated; 90 minutes)

T99   *Live from Lincoln Center: Beverly! Her Farewell Performance* (27 October 1980; PBS)

Merman, one of many guests who honored Beverly Sills at her retirement from singing, performed "There's No Business Like Show Business." Mary Martin was also on the bill.

T100   *Inaugural Celebration of Ronald Reagan* (19 January 1981; ABC; 120 minutes)

T101   *Showstoppers* (1981; HBO)

Merman sang "I Get a Kick out of You" and "There's No Business Like Show Business."

T102   *100 Years of America's Popular Music* (27 Apr. 1981; NBC)

George Burns was the host of this program. Merman sang a medley with Gordon MacRae.

T103   *The Love Boat* (10 Oct. 1981; ABC; 60 minutes)

T104   *Night of 100 Stars* (8 Mar. 1982; ABC; 180 minutes)

This program, taped at Radio City Music Hall on 14 Feb. 1982, was a benefit for the Actors' Fund. The executive producer was Alexander H. Cohen; the producer, Hildy Parks; the director, Clark Jones; the announcer, Les Marshack; the musical director, Elliot Lawrence; the musical stager, Albert Stevenson; the writer, Hildy Parks; and the art director, Charles Lisanby. Merman sang "There's No Business Like Show Business."

T105   *The Love Boat: The Musical* (27 February 1982; ABC; 60 minutes)

Appearing once again as "Rosie Smith," Merman sang "What I Did for Love," "Everything's Coming up Roses," and "I'm the Greatest Star."

T106   *The Tonight Show* (7 May 1982; NBC; 105 minutes)

T107   *The Merv Griffin Show* (25 May 1982; Syndicated; 90 minutes)

Griffin celebrated Merman's concert at Carnegie Hall and her receipt of ASCAP's Pied Piper Award. Also on the show were Ginger Rogers, Lucille Ball, Jule Style, Hal David, and Jerry Herman.

T108   *The Tonight Show* (19 May 1982; NBC; 105 minutes)

Merman's numbers were "Everything's Coming up Roses" and "I'm the Greatest Star."

T109   *Texaco Star Theater: Opening Night* (11 September 1982; NBC; 90 minutes)

The executive producer was Marty Pasetta; the producer, Kenny Solms; the director, Marty Pasetta; the musical director, Billy Byers; the musical supervisors, Artie Malvin and Stan Freeman; the writers, Ann Elder, Fritz Holt, and Kenny Solms; the art directors, Ray Klausen and Bob Rang; and the choreographer, Artie Johnson. Merman contributed "There's No Business Like Show Business" and "Anything You Can Do, I Can Do Better."

T110   *Royal Command Variety Performance* (8 November 1982; BBC)

Merman dominated the finale with "There's No Business Like Show Business."

T111   *Over Easy* with Mary Martin (1982: PBS)

T112   *The Monte Carlo Show* (1982; Syndicated; 60 minutes)

Merman sang "the medley" on this variety show with Patrick Wayne as the host.

T113   *Broadway: A Special Salute* (4 May 1985; PBS)

Originally taped earlier for The Entertainment Channel, Merman appeared with Mary Martin, Chita Rivera, Nell Carter, Jerry Orbach, and others.

This list is by no means complete. In addition to numerous appearances on *The Muppet Show* and frequent interviews on national and local talk shows, Merman was seen on *The Match Game*, *Sha Na Na*, *The Hollywood Squares*, *The Bobby Vinton Show*, *Kids Are People Too*, and *The Polly Bergen Show*. She also made commercials for Canada Dry, Vell, Texaco, and Friendship Cottage Cheese. The reader is further advised that in the case of some syndicated programs, the dates may represent filming rather than airing times.

Discography

D01 *Follow the Leader* (Paramount; 1930)

This is a studio soundtrack recording of a film made by Merman and Ginger Rogers while they were appearing on stage in *Girl Crazy*. The song "Satan's Holiday" from this sound-track was released on Encore Records' *Merman in the Movies* (ST 101).

D02 *Ireno* (Paramount; 1931)

A short film made by Merman in 1931, *Ireno* contains Merman's rendition of "Wipe That Frown Right off Your Face," which was released by Take Two Records on *Legends of the Musical Stage* (TT 104).

D03 "Life Is Just a Bowl of Cherries"/"My Song"/ "Ladies and Gentlemen, That's Love"

These songs from *George White's Scandals* were recorded by Merman in October 1931, but Victor never released them.

D04 "How Deep Is the Ocean?"/"I'll Follow You"
"Satan's Little Lamb"/"I Gotta Right to Sing the Blues"

Victor recorded these sides on 28 September 1932 and released them as 78 rpm singles (Victor 24146 and 24145). They were later reissued on the "X" Vault Originals label (LVA 1004). "How Deep Is the Ocean?" appears on the RCA Camden *Great Personalities of Broadway* LP album as well as *The Vintage Berlin* (New World NW 238).

D05   *Ethel Merman (1932-1935)-Lyda Roberti (1934)-Mae West (1933)* (Columbia Records; 1967) Mono CL 2751

Merman recorded these songs for the Brunswick label in the early 1930s: "Eadie Was a Lady" (#6456, recorded 16 December 1932); "An Earful of Music" (#6995, recorded 8 October 1934); "I Get a Kick out of You"/"You're the Top" (recorded 4 December 1934); "The Lady in Red"/"It's the Animal in Me" (#7491, recorded 17 July 1935).

Reviews: See **B201, B202.**

D06   *Ethel Merman Sings Cole Porter* (JJC Records) M 3004; reissued as AEI 1147

Merman's original 78 rpm singles of these songs were originally recorded for the Liberty Music Shop (New York): "Down in the Depths"/"It's De-Lovely" (#206, recorded 6 Nov. 1936); "Ridin' High"/"Red, Hot, and Blue" (#207, recorded 6 November 1936); "A Lady Needs a Change"/"I'll Pay the Check" (#256, recorded 22 Feb. 1939); "This Is It"/"Just a Little Bit More" (#257, recorded 22 February 1939).

D07   *We're not Dressing* (Paramount; 1934)

This studio soundtrack recording includes "It's Just a New Spanish Custom," sung by Merman and Leon Errol, which was released by Encore Records, *Merman in the Movies* (ST 101). "He Reminds Me of You," originally recorded as a Paramount promotional disc, was issued in *Personalities on Parade*, Vol. 2 (No label PP-2).

D08   *Kid Millions* (Goldwyn; 1934)

Merman's songs for this film include "An Earful of Music," "Mandy," and "Ice Cream Fantasy." The soundtrack recordings were issued on Classic International Filmusicals CIF 3007 (mono) and Sandy Hook SH 2039.

D09   *The Big Broadcast of 1936* (Paramount; 1935)

Merman's "It's the Animal in Me" was originally filmed for *We're not Dressing* and later released by Encore Records, *Merman in the Movies* (ST 101).

D10   *Anything Goes* (Paramount; 1936)

Merman is heard singing "Anything Goes" under the main titles; this version was released on Caliban 6053. She also sang "I Get a Kick out of You" and (with Bing Crosby) "You're the Top" and "Shanghai-De-Ho," later issued as Encore Records, *Merman in the Movies* (ST 101).

D11   *Strike Me Pink* (Goldwyn; 1936)

"First You Have Me High, Then You Have Me Low" and "Calabash Pipe" (with Eddie Cantor) were among Merman's contributions to this film. They were released on Encore Records, *Merman in the Movies* (ST 101).

D12   *Happy Landing* (Twentieth Century-Fox; 1938)

Merman sang "Hot and Happy" and "You Appeal to Me" in this film; they appear on Encore Records, *Merman in the Movies* (ST 101). Her recording of "You Are the Music to the Words in

My Heart" was excised from the final version of the film but is included in the Encore release.

D13   *Straight, Place and Show* (Twentieth Century-Fox; 1938)

For this film Merman performed "With You on My Mind" and "Why not String Along with Me?". Both are on Encore Records, *Merman in the Movies* (ST 101), but the version of the latter number on Choice Cuts ST 500/1 is a fuller rendition. They are also on Vertinge 2000.

D14   *Alexander's Ragtime Band* (Twentieth Century-Fox; 1938)

This film includes Merman's versions of "Say It with Music," "A Pretty Girl Is Like a Melody," "Blue Skies" (with Alice Faye), "Pack up Your Sins and Go to the Devil," "My Walking Stick," "Everybody Step," and "Heat Wave." They were issued on Hollywood Soundstage 406, and some selections are on Encore Records, *Merman in the Movies* (ST 101).

D15   "I Surrender, Dear"

Merman sang this song on the radio on 15 December 1932. It appears on *The Thirties Girls*, Sandy Hook (SH 2027).

D16   "Marching Along with Time"

Also recorded on a radio broadcast (20 September 1938), this number is on *Girls of the '30s* (Pelican LP 122).

D17   "It's All Yours"

Merman sang this duet with Jimmy Durante on radio in 1939. It can be heard on *Forgotten Broadway*, Vol. 2 (T102).

D18 "Friendship"

Bert Lahr joins Merman for this duet recorded from a radio broadcast in 1940. It is included in *Stars over Broadway*, Star Tone (ST 214).

D19 *Panama Hattie* (Decca Records; 1940)

Opened 30 October 1940 at the 46th Street Theatre, New York. Music and lyrics; Cole Porter. Musical direction: Harry Sosnick.

"Let's Be Buddies" (with Joan Carroll)/"Make It Another Old-Fashioned, Please" was released as Decca 23199; Decca 23200 featured "My Mother Would Love You"/"I've Still Got My Health." All four were reissued on LP in *Cole Porter: 1924-1944* (JJA 19732).

D20 "I'm Throwing a Ball Tonight"/"Make It Another Old-Fashioned, Please"

These live performances of songs from *Panama Hattie* were released on *Cole Porter* (JJA 19745).

D21 "Marching through Berlin"

Merman sang this song in the film *Stage Door Canteen*. This version appears on *Stage Door Canteen/Hollywood Canteen* (Curtain Calls 100/11-2) and Sandy Hook SH 2093. She recorded another version accompanied by a male quartet, released as Victor 20-2521, with "Move It Over" on the flip side.

D22 "Why Do They Call a Private a Private?" V-Disc 368A

This disc was recorded as part of a live performance in aid of the war effort.

D23 *Something for the Boys* (AEI Records; 1943) AEI 1157

Opened on 7 January 1943 at the Alvin Theatre, New York. Music and lyrics: Cole Porter. Musical direction: William Parson and David Broekman.

Merman's songs in this album, which was recorded from a radio broadcast, are "Something for the Boys," "Hey, Good Lookin'" (with Bill Johnson), "He's a Right Guy," "I'm in Love with a Soldier Boy," "There's a Happy Land in the Sky" (with Allen Jenkins and Bill Johnson), "By the Mississinewah" (with Betty Bruce), and "Finale" (with ensemble). Sound/Stage Records (2305) issued a somewhat different version.

D24   *Annie Get Your Gun* (Decca Records; 1946) DL 8001; reissued as MCA 1626

Opened on 17 May 1946 at the Imperial Theatre, New York. Music and lyrics: Irving Berlin. Musical direction: Jay Blackton.

Merman's numbers include "Doin' What Comes Natur'lly," "Moonshine Lullaby" (with Leon Bibb, John Garth, and Clyde Turner), "You Can't Get a Man with a Gun," "I'm an Indian Too," "They Say It's Wonderful" (with Ray Middleton), "Anything You Can Do" (with Ray Middleton), "I Got Lost in His Arms," and "I Got the Sun in the Morning."

D25   *Ethel Merman: Songs She Has Made Famous* (Decca Records; 1947) DL 5053 (mono)

This album, recorded in December 1947 under the musical direction of Jay Blackton, features "You're the Top," "I Get a Kick out of You," "Eadie Was a Lady," "Blow, Gabriel, Blow," "I Got Rhythm," "It's De-Lovely," and "Life Is Just a Bowl of Cherries."

D26   *Call Me Madam* (Decca Records; 1950) DL 8035 (mono); reissued as MCA 1532

Opened on 12 Oct. 1950 at the Imperial Theatre in New York. Music and lyrics: Irving Berlin. Musical direction: Gordon Jenkins.

RCA released the "original cast" album with Dinah Shore as Sally Adams because Merman was under exclusive contract to Decca. Merman, however, recorded and Decca released her songs from the show: "The Hostess with the Mostes' on the Ball," "Washington Square Dance," "Can You Use Any Money Today?," "Marrying for Love," "The Best Thing for You," "Something to Dance About," and "You're Just in Love" (with Dick Haymes).

D27 "You're Just in Love" (with Russell Nye)

This duet from *Call Me Madam* with her original partner was probably recorded from a radio broadcast and released in *Original Performances from the Best of Broadway Musicals* (Columbia House P6S 5936).

D28 *Ethel Merman: The World Is Your Balloon* (MCA [British]) MCA 1839

Several of the duets in this album were released as singles by Decca Records in the 1950s: "A Little Girl from Little Rock," "Diamonds Are a Girl's Best Friend," "Dearie" (with Ray Bolger), "I Said My Pajamas" (with Ray Bolger), "It's So Nice to Have a Man around the House" (with Ray Bolger), "(If I Knew You Were Comin') I'd've Baked a Cake" (with Ray Bolger), "Calico Sal," "She's Shimmyin' on the Beach Again," "Hawaii," "Ukulele Lady," "The Lake Song" (with Ray Bolger), "Don't Believe It" (with Ray Bolger), "Once upon a Nickel" (with Ray Bolger), "Oldies" (with Ray Bolger), "Love Is the Reason," "The World Is Your Balloon," "Make the Man Love Me," "You Say the Nicest Things" (with Jimmy Durante), "A Husband--A Wife" (with Jimmy

Durante), and "If You Catch a Little Cold" (with Jimmy Durante).

D29   *Call Me Madam* (Twentieth Century-Fox; 1953) Decca 5465 (mono), reissued as Ster DS 25001

Music and lyrics: Irving Berlin. Musical direction: Alfred Newman. Again Merman sings "The Hostess with the Mostes' on the Ball," "Can You Use Any Money Today?," "The International Rag," "You're Just in Love" (with Donald O'Connor), "The Best Thing for You" (with George Sanders), Finale: "You're Just in Love" (with George Sanders) and "Something to Dance About" (with George Sanders).

D30   *Ethel Merman and Mary Martin Duet from the Ford 50th Anniversary TV Show* (Decca Records; 1953) DL 7027 (mono)

This historic duet was recorded from a live television special broadcast on 15 June 1953. The number lasted for only twelve minutes, but it was a veritable retrospection of the singers' illustrious careers that featured "I" songs: Fanfare (orchestra, directed by Jay Blackton), "There's No Business Like Show Business" (Merman), "A Wonderful Guy" (Martin), "By the Light of the Silvery Moon" (Merman), "Wait Till the Sun Shines, Nellie" (Martin), "The Sheik of Araby" (Merman), "When the Red, Red Robin Comes Bob, Bob, Bobbing Along" (both), "Mississippi Mud" (Martin), "I Cried for You" (Merman), "I'm Forever Blowing Bubbles" (Martin), "I'm Always Chasing Rainbows" (Merman), "I'm in the Mood for Love" (Martin), "I Love a Parade" (Merman), "I'd Climb the Highest Mountain" (Martin), "I'm Sitting on Top of the World" (Merman), "I've Got a Feelin' You're Foolin'" (Martin), "I Can't Give You Anything but Love" (Merman), "I'll Get By" (Martin), "You're Just in Love" (Merman), "I'm Gonna Wash That Man Right outa My

Hair" (Martin), "I Get a Kick out of You" (Merman), "I've Got You under My Skin" (Martin), "My Heart Belongs to Daddy" (Martin), "I Got Rhythm" (Merman), "Indian Love Call" (Martin), "Tea for Two" (both), "Stormy Weather" (Merman), "I Got Rhythm" (Merman), "Isn't It Romantic?" (Martin), "There's No Business Like Show Business" (both).

D31 *There's No Business Like Show Business* (Twentieth Century-Fox; 1954) Decca DL 8091 (mono)

Music and lyrics: Irving Berlin. Musical direction: Alfred Newman and Lionel Newman. Merman's songs are "There's No Business Like Show Business," "When the Midnight Choo-Choo Leaves for Alabam'" (with Dan Dailey), "Play a Simple Melody" (with Dan Dailey), "A Sailor's not a Sailor" (with Mitzi Gaynor), and "Alexander's Ragtime Band" (with Dan Dailey, Mitzi Gaynor, Donald O'Connor, and Johnnie Ray).

D32 *Memories: 40 Great Songs from the Gay '90s to the Roaring '20s* (Decca Records) DL 9028

Musical direction: Jay Blackton. Merman sings with the assistance of the Mitchell Boys' Choir and the Old Timers' Quartet "The Band Played On," "The Bowery," "On a Saturday Night," "While Strolling through the Park One Day," "I've Got Rings on My Fingers," "In My Merry Oldsmobile," "In the Good Old Summertime," "Waltz Me Around Again, Willie," "On a Bicycle Built for Two," "She Be Comin' 'Round the Mountain," "Put on Your Old Gray Bonnet," "M-I-S-S-I-S-S-I-P-P-I," "Listen to the Mocking Bird," "You Tell Me Your Dream (I'll Tell You Mine)," "School Days," "Memories," "Way Down Yonder in New Orleans," "Somebody Stole My Gal," "Smiles," "Sweet Georgia Brown," "Take Back Your Gold," "Frankie and Johnny," "On Moonlight Bay," "By the Light of the Silv'ry Moon," "Shine On, Harvest Moon," "That Old Gang of Mine," "Sweet Adeline," "Oh, John- ny, Oh, Johnny, Oh!," "Dear Little Boy of Mine," "Forty-Five Minutes from Broadway," "Mary's a Grand Old Name," and "Give My Regards to Broadway."

D33 *Ethel Merman: A Musical Autobiography* (Decca Records; 1956) DX 153

Musical direction: Buddy Cole. A narrative spoken by Merman links this collection of songs that spans her career: "I Got Rhythm," "Embraceable You," "Life Is Just a Bowl of Cherries," "Eadie Was a Lady," "You're an Old Smoothie," "Anything Goes," "Blow, Gabriel, Blow," "I Get a Kick out of You," "You're the Top," "It's De-Lovely," "Ridin' High," "Down in the Depths on the 90th Floor," "This Is It," "I'll Pay the Check," "Do I Love You," "Friendship," "Let's Be Buddies" (with Joan Carroll), "Make It Another Old-Fashioned, Please," "He's a Right Guy," "Doin' What Comes Natur'lly," "Moonshine Lullaby" (with Leon Bibb, John Garth, and Clyde Turner), "You Can't Get a Man with a Gun," "I'm an Indian Too," "They Say It's Wonderful" (with Ray Mid- dleton), "I Got Lost in His Arms," "I Got the Sun in the Morning," "The Hostess with the Mostes' on the Ball," "Washington Square Dance," "You're Just in Love" (with Dick Haymes), "The Best Thing for You," "Something to Dance About," "Alexander's Ragtime Band," "Dearie" (with Ray Bolger), and "How Deep Is the Ocean?."

D34 *Anything Goes* (Larynx 567; reissued as Sandy Hook Records; 1981) SH 2043 (mono)

Music and lyrics: Cole Porter. Musical direc- tion: Al Goodman. This mutilated version of Merman's show of 1934 was broadcasted on TV's *The Colgate Comedy Hour* on 28 February 1954. Merman is assisted by Frank Sinatra, Bert

Lahr, Sheree North, and Al Goodman's Orches-
tra. Merman sings "Anything Goes," "You Do
Something to Me" (with Sinatra), "I Get a Kick
out of You," "You're the Top," "Just One of
Those Things," "Blow, Gabriel, Blow," and
"Friendship."

D35 *Panama Hattie* (Larynx 557; reissued as
Sandy Hook Records; 1981) SH 2043 (mono)

Music and lyrics: Cole Porter. Musical direction: Buster Davis. Merman reprises her show
of 1940 in this version telecast on *The Best
of Broadway* on 10 November 1954. In the cast
are Ray Middleton, Art Carney, and Jack E.
Leonard. Merman's songs are "Ridin' High,"
"I'm in Love," "Let's Be Buddies," and "Make
It Another Old-Fashioned, Please."

D36 *Happy Hunting* (RCA Victor; 1956) LOC-
1026 (mono)

Opened on 6 Dec. 1956 at the Alvin Theatre,
New York. Music: Harold Karr. Lyrics: Howard
Lind-say. Musical direction: Jay Blackton.
Merman's songs are "It's Good to Be Here,"
"Mutual Admiration Society" (with Virginia
Gibson), "Mr. Livingstone," "This Is What I
Call Love," "A New-Fangled Tango" (with Vir-
ginia Gibson and Leon Belasco, "The Game of
Love," "Happy Hunting," "I'm a Funny Dame"
(with Fernando Lamas), and "Grand Finale."

D37 *Gypsy* (Columbia Records; 1959) OS 2017
(stereo)

Opened on 21 May 1959 at the Broadway Theatre,
New York. Music: Jule Styne. Lyrics: Stephen
Sondheim. Musical direction: Milton Rosen-
stock. Merman scintillates in "Some People,"
"Small World" (with Jack Klugman), "Mr. Gold-
stone, I Love You," "You'll Never Get Away
from Me" (with Jack Klugman), "Everything's
Coming up Roses," "Together" (with Sandra

Church and Jack Klugman), and the incomparable "Rose's Turn."

D38   *Forgotten Broadway, Vol. II*, T102

Merman sings "Little Lamb," but the jacket notes indicate none of the circumstances of the recording.

D39   *The Lindsay Record* (Columbia Records) CSP 261

Musical direction: Harold Hastings. Merman supported John Lindsay's candidacy for mayor of New York by singing special Sondheim lyrics to "Everything's Coming up Roses."

D40   *Merman...Her Greatest!* (Reprise; 1961) R-6032 (stereo); reissued as Stanyan 10070

Musical direction: Billy May. Assisted by May's buoyant, modern orchestrations, Merman reinterprets her classics: "I Got Rhythm," "This Is It," "Do I Love You?," "Sam and Delilah," "Life Is Just a Bowl of Cherries," "Blow, Gabriel, Blow," "You're an Old Smoothie," "Down in the Depths on the 90th Floor," "But not for Me," "Friendship," and "You're the Top."

D41   "It's De-Lovely" (with Bob Hope)

This duet, recorded from a television broadcast in 1956, was released on *Cole Porter* (JJA 19745).

D42   *Merman in Vegas* (Reprise; Oct. 1962) R9-6062 (stereo)

Musical direction: Russ Black. Arrangements: Billy May. Merman opened at the Flamingo in Las Vegas on 25 October 1962. Her numbers included "Just a Lady with a Song," "I Got Rhythm," "This Is It," "A Lot of Livin' to Do," Medley: "Doin' What Comes Natur'lly," "The Hostess with the Mostes' on the Ball," "I Got the Sun in the Morning," "Life Is Just a Bowl of Cherries," "You're the Top," "You're an Old Smoothie," "Let's Be Buddies," "Anything Goes," "It's De-Lovely," "Small World," "Everything's Coming up Roses"; "They Say It's Wonderful," "Make It Another Old-Fashioned, Please," "You Can't Get a Man with a Gun," "Blow, Gabriel, Blow," and "There's No Business Like Show Business."

D43 *Journey Back to Oz* (Filmation; recorded 1962, released 1974) RFO 101 (stereo) as *The Return to Oz*

Only Merman's voice is heard in this film. She sings "Be a Witch," "Keep a Gloomy Thought," and "An Elephant Never Forgets."

D44 *The Judy Garland Show* (Kismet; 6 October 1963) 1002 (mono)

The album was released as *Looking Back* and featured Merman singing "There's No Business Like Show Business" with Judy Garland and Barbra Streisand.

D45 *The Judy Garland Show* (Broadcast Tributes; 12 January 1964) BTRIB 0002 as *The Greatest Duets*; Paragon 1001 as *Great Garland Duets* (mono)

Musical direction: Mort Lindsey. Merman and Garland sing a medley of "Friendship," "Let's Be Buddies," "You're the Top," "You're Just in Love," "It's De-Lovely," and "Together."

D46 *Annie Get Your Gun* (RCA Victor; 1966) Mono LOC-1124, Stereo LSO-1124

Opened on 31 May 1966 at the New York State Theatre. Music and Lyrics: Irving Berlin.

Musical direction: Franz Allers. In this original cast recording, Merman sings a new song written especially for this revival, "An Old Fashioned Wedding" (with Bruce Yarnell), as well as the ones she had made famous two decades earlier: "Doin' What Comes Natur'lly" (with Ronn Carroll), "You Can't Get a Man with a Gun," "There's No Business Like Show Business" (with Bruce Yarnell and Rufus Smith), "They Say It's Wonderful" (with Bruce Yarnell), "Moonshine Lullaby," "I'm an Indian Too," "I Got Lost in His Arms," "I Got the Sun in the Morning," and "Anything You Can Do" (with Bruce Yarnell).

D47   *Ethel Merman Sings the New Songs from Hello, Dolly!* (Bar-Mic Records; 1970) no number (stereo)

Music and Lyrics: Jerry Herman. Merman, with an instrumental trio, sings the songs originally written for her but not inserted in the show until she assumed the role of Dolly Levi on 28 March 1970: "Love, Look in My Window" and "World, Take Me Back."

D48   *Merman Sings Merman* (London Records; 1972) XPS-901 (stereo)

Musical direction: Stanley Black. With the assistance of the London Festival Orchestra and Chorus, Merman sings "You're the Top," "I Got Rhythm," "You're Just in Love," "Alexander's Ragtime Band," "I Got Lost in His Arms," "Eadie Was a Lady," "There's No Business Like Show Business," "They Say It's Wonderful," "It's D'Lovely," "I Get a Kick out of You," "Everything's Coming up Roses," and "Blow, Gabriel, Blow."

D49   *Annie Get Your Gun* (London Records; 1973) XPS-905 (stereo)

Music and lyrics: Irving Berlin. Musical direction: Stanley Black. For the contents of this recording, see **D46**.

D50 *Ethel's Ridin' High* (London Records; 1974) PS 909 (stereo)

Musical direction: Stanley Black. Again in league with the London Festival Orchestra and Chorus, Merman vocalizes on "Gee, But It's Good to Be Here," "Whispering," "Some People," "People," "Sunrise, Sunset," "What Kind of Fool Am I?," "Ridin' High," "Someone to Watch over Me," "The Impossible Dream," "On a Clear Day," and "Nothing Can Stop Me Now."

D51 *A Gala Tribute to Joshua Logan* (no label, no number)

Merman sings a medley that includes "The Parts I've Played," "Doin' What Comes Natur'lly," "The Hostess with the Mostes' on the Ball," "I Got the Sun in the Morning," "Life Is Just a Bowl of Cherries," spoken narrative about Gershwin, "I Got Rhythm," "You're an Old Smoothie," "Let's Be Buddies," "Anything Goes," "It's De-Lovely," "Small World," "Everything's Coming up Roses." The rest of the cast joins Merman for a finale of "There's No Business Like Show Business."

D52 *Together on Broadway* (no label, no number)

Musical direction: Jay Blackton. Merman's conductor: Eric Knight. Merman sings "Send in the Clowns" (with Mary Martin), Medley, "It's Good to Be Here," "Blow, Gabriel, Blow," "Hello, Dolly!" (with Mary Martin), the Ford TV Duet (see **D30**, with Mary Martin), "There's No Business Like Show Business" (with entire cast).

D53 *The Ethel Merman Disco Album* (A & M Records; 1979) SP 4775 (stereo)

Musical direction and arrangements: Peter Matz. Merman interpreted her classics in her usual manner, but disco rhythms were added in the studio: "There's No Business Like Show Business," "Everything's Coming up Roses," "I Get a Kick out of You," "Something for the Boys," "Alexander's Ragtime Band," and "I Got Rhythm." Unfortunately for sales, the album was released at the end of the disco period.

<u>Review</u>: See **B43**.

D54   *Ethel Merman at Carnegie Hall* (no label, no number)

Musical direction: Eric Knight. This concert in aid of the City Museum of New York included "A Lady with a Song," "It's Good to Be Here," Medley, "They Say It's Wonderful," "Some People," "Alexander's Ragtime Band," "I Get a Kick out of You," "Blow, Gabriel, Blow," "There's No Business Like Show Business," "What I Did for Love," and "Someone to Watch over Me."

D55   *Greetings from Broadway*   (AEI)   1176 (mono)

Merman's rendition of "Have Yourself a Merry Little Christmas," recorded for a Perry Como television show in 1959, is on this album.

Bibliography

B01   Abbott, George. *"Mister Abbott."*
New York: Random House, 1963. pp.
226-228

Abbott as director of *Call Me Madam*
speaks of his vain attempts to persuade Merman
to look at Paul Lukas during their scenes.

B02   "Actor Appealing Equity's Censure."
New York Times 25 Dec. 1957: A36,
1-2.

This article, as well as **B03**, **B124**, **B138**,
B227, and **B541**, deals with the Gene Wesson affair.

B03   "Actress Fights Call: Ethel Merman
against Subpoena in Actor's Suit."
New York Times 8 Apr. 1958: A32,
5.

B04   Adams, Joey and Henry Tobias. *The
Borscht Belt*. Indianapolis: Bobbs-
Merrill, 1966. p. 94

Adams writes of Abner J. ("Abby") Gresh-
ler, a booking agent for the "borscht" circuit
of resort hotels, and his enterprising scheme
for luring entertainers, such as Merman, onto

the stages of hotels at which he had registered them as guests.

B05   ------------. *Here's to the Friars:*
               The Heart of Show Business. New
               York: Crown Publishers, 1976. pp.
               63, 156

B06   Adler, Larry. *It Ain't Necessarily*
               So: An Autobiography.   New York:
               Grove Press, pp. 16, 31, 49

Adler was in agent Lou Irwin's office
when Merman loudly insisted that Irwin win her
release from her film contract with Warner
Brothers. "One thing I have never understood,"
he writes. "No show then had amplification.
Performers like Al Jolson or Eddie Cantor
didn't need mikes and Ethel Merman could have
been heard two blocks away."

B07   Agee, James. "Films." Rev. of *Stage*
               Door Canteen. *Nation* 156 (12 June
               1943): 844.

This critic does not evaluate Merman's
performance.

B08   Alpert, Hollis.   *Broadway!: 45*
               Years of Musical Theatre.   New
               York: Arcade Publishing Company,
               1991. pp. 99, 106, 107-109, 119,
               120, 121, 151, 153-154, 196, 198-
               199, 201, 209

B09   Anderson, John. "Red, Hot, and
               Blue!" Rev. of *Red, Hot, and Blue!*.
               (NY) *Journal* 31 Oct. 1936.

"There is Miss Merman, as shiny as ever
and as suavely clever in putting over her
songs, even if they do not seem worth the
trouble."

B10 --------------. "Stars in Your Eyes." Rev. of *Stars in Your Eyes.* (NY) *Journal-American* 10 Feb. 1939.

B11 Anderson, Susan H. "Ethel Merman." *International Herald-Tribune* 30 May 1980.

B12 "Another Play." Rev. of *Girl Crazy.* (NY) *World* 15 Oct. 1930.

Merman's numbers were delivered, according to the reviewer, "with abandon and conviction that brought new technique to the school of contralto shouts and upraised rhythmic arms."

B13 "Anything Goes--and Often Does." Rev. of *Anything Goes. Literary Digest* 118 (8 Dec. 1934): 18.

In this her fourth Broadway show, Merman is already called the "queen of musical comedy."

B14 "Anything Goes Again." *Life* 36 (15 Mar. 1954): 91-92.

B15 Argus. "On the Current Screen." Rev. of *We're not Dressing. Literary Digest* 117 (12 May 1934): 34.

The film achieves "a delicate balance between plot and music," and Merman helps to keep the piece "mildly hilarious." The article includes a photograph of her.

B16 "ASCAP Honors Miss Merman as Its Pied Piper." *New York Times* 13 Feb. 1982: A18, 3-5.

B17 Aston, Frank. "*Gypsy*, Ethel Smash Hits." Rev. of *Gypsy. New World*

Telegram   22 May 1959, in *New York Theatre Critics' Reviews* 1959: 302.

B18   Atkinson, Brooks. *Broadway*. New York: Macmillan, 1970. pp. 322, 324, 326, 330, 385

B19   ----------------. *Broadway Scrapbook*. New York: Theatre Arts, 1947; rept. Westport, CT: Greenwood Press, 1970. pp. 235, 237-240

B20   ----------------. "First Night at the Theatre." Rev. of *Call Me Madam*. *New York Times* 13 Oct. 1950: A25, 1.

Merman "is still lighting up like an inspired pin-ball machine, and still blowing the music lustily throughout the theatre. . . . We were all eating out of Ethel's hand last evening, for she was acting in the grand manner without being snobbish or pretentious."

B21   ----------------.   "Jack Haley, Ethel Merman and a Rowdy Musical Evening." Rev. of *Take a Chance*. *New York Times* 28 Nov. 1932:   A11, 2.

B22   ----------------. "The Play." Rev. of *Du Barry Was a Lady*. *New York Times*   7 Dec. 1939: A34, 2-3.

After complaining of the vulgarity of the piece, Atkinson adds, "Fortunately, Miss Merman and Mr. Lahr are the people to make vulgarity honestly exuberant."

B23   ----------------. "The Play." Rev. of *George White's Scandals*.   *New York Times* 15 Sept. 1931: K30.

Merman's voice is described as "inexhaustible" and the lady herself as the "Queen of the singing announcers."

B24   ----------------. "The Play." Rev. of *Panama Hattie*. *New York Times* 31 Oct. 1940: A28, 2.

"Nothing new to say of Miss Merman. She is singing especially well, and looking particularly fresh and lovely, and she makes a thorough job of her assignment, as is her custom." She is like a "high-compression engine: She rolls through it with the greatest gusto, giving it a shake and a gleam and plenty of syncopation."

B25   ----------------. "The Play." Rev. of *Red, Hot, and Blue!*. *New York Times* 31 Oct. 1936: L24.

Merman "is still the most commanding minstrel in the business, wearing her costumes like a drum major, swinging to the music and turning the audience into a congregation of pals for the evening."

B26   ----------------. "The Play." Rev. of *Stars in Your Eyes*. *New York Times* 10 Feb. 1939: A18, 2, 3.

"Let Ethel Merman and Jimmy Durante step forward and receive any prizes that might be handy. . . they give the gutsiest performances of their careers. . . . Merman has had a way with a song for a long time. Give her a tune and she takes complete charge of it, not forgetting to pronounce the words. . . . She knows comedy as thoroughly as she knows singing. . . ."

B27   ----------------. "Theatre: Good Show!" Rev. of *Gypsy*. *New York Times* 22 May 1959: A31, 6.

"Since Ethel Merman is the head woman in Gypsy. . . nothing can go wrong."

B28   ----------------. "Theatre: Return of Ethel Merman." Rev. of *Happy Hunting*. *New York Times*   7 Dec. 1956: A30, 1.

"The explosion on 44th Street last night was nothing to be alarmed by. It was merely Ethel Merman returning to the New York theatre. . . ."

B29   Bacon, James. *How Sweet It Is: The Jackie Gleason Story*. New York: St. Martin's Press, 1985. pp. 55, 72

B30   Bankhead, Tallulah. *Tallulah: My Autobiography*. New York: Harper and Brothers, 1952. pp. 291, 292, 295

B31   Baral, Robert. *Revue: The Great Broadway Period*. New York: Fleet Press, 1962. pp. 24, 144, 145, 196

Clearly an avid supporter of Merman, Baral gives a show-by-show description of her revue-like vehicles.

B32   Barnes, Clive. "La Merman at Carnegie Hall Still and Simply the Very Best." *New York Post*, 11 May 1982.

Addressing Merman, Barnes says, "You were a strange muse for the likes of George Gershwin, Cole Porter, Irving Berlin, and Jule Styne. You also became the embodiment of musical comedy when people knew what musical comedy was. Your voice was the clarion call for a kind of theatre--and . . . what a clarion!"

B33   Barnes, Howard. "Bull's Eye." Rev. of *Annie Get Your Gun*. *The Theatres* May 1946.

". . . the one and only Ethel Merman struts through the proceedings with such exuberant enchantment that the show would have been memorable even without its meticulous and impressive panoply. . . ."

B34   --------------. "Call Me Madam." Rev. of *Call Me Madam*. *The Theatres* 13 Oct. 1950 in *New York Theatre Critics' Reviews* 1950: 245.

"Miss Merman has a way of setting off the cavortings of song and dance nonsense with distinction."

B35   ------------. "Return of Queen Ethel--and Some Lesser Matters." Rev. of *Happy Hunting*. *The Theatres* Dec. 1956.

"The presence of Ethel Merman in a musical show disarms criticism. . . ."

B36   Barthel, Joan. "Out Comes Ethel Naturally." *New York Times* 29 May 1966: B1, 4-6.

B37   Baxter, Beverley. *First Nights and Footlights*. London: Hutchinson, 1955. p. 159.

Having seen and liked Broadway's *Call Me Madam*, critic Baxter compares the performance of Billie Worth in the London production with Merman's: "Miss Billie Worth has charm and humour, whereas Ethel Merman relies on a vitality that dominates the New York production like a cyclone."

B38   "Belated Arrival." *New York Times*
               12 May 1946: B2, 2.

The picture of Merman in costume heralds
the advent of *Annie Get Your Gun*.

B39   "Benefit for Fund Is Held at
               Barney's Department Store: Celeb-
               rities Attending Include Ethel
               Merman." *New York Times* 25 Sept.
               1979: B9, 1.

B40   Bergreen, Laurence. *As Thousands
               Cheer: The Life of Irving Berlin*.
               New York: Viking, 1990.   pp. 362-
               363, 376, 447, 453, 456-458, 471,
               498-500, 502-507, 508, 514, 518-
               519, 523, 533, 550, 554-556, 575

B41   Berle, Milton. *B. S. I Love You:
               60 Funny Years with the Famous and
               the Infamous*. New York: McGraw-
               Hill, 1988. p. 162

Berle quotes Oscar Levant: "Irving Berlin
can't write a bad song for Ethel Merman. If he
does, you'll hear it."

B42   ------------- and Haskel Frankel.
               Milton Berle: An Autobiography. New
               York: Delacorte Press, 1974. pp.
               134, 290

B43   Bernstein, Fred. "On the Move:
               Don't Worry about the Size of Ethel
               Merman's Belt: At 70 She's Record-
               ing Disco." *People* 12 (24 Sept.
               1979): 55-56.

The release of *The Ethel Merman Disco Album* prompted this interview. Singer Donna Summer attended the recording session and said to
Merman, "If I'm the Queen of Disco, you're the
Disco Diva."

B44   Bill. Rev. of *The Bob Hope Show*.
Variety 28 Mar. 1962: A34, 1.

B45   Bissell, Richard. "Manic Musical
Comedy." Rev. of *Happy Hunting*.
Holiday 22 (Aug. 1957): 45.

B46   Black, Shirley Temple. *Child Star:*
An Autobiography. New York: Warner
Books, 1988. pp. 326, 332, 373, 500

Black recalls negotiations for her to
play the child's role in *Panama Hattie*.

B47   Blum, Daniel. *Great Stars of the*
American Stage: A Pictorial Record.
New York: Grosset and Dunlap, 1954.
pp. 121-122

B48   ----------- and John Willis. *A*
Pictorial History of the American
Theatre 1860-1970. 3rd ed. New
York: Crown Publishers, 1969. pp.
249, 254, 257, 258, 265, 275, 285,
286, 289, 290, 298, 301, 310, 314,
330, 331, 358, 368, 376

B49   Boehnel, William. "*Girl Crazy* Makes
Hit as Diverting New Show." Rev. of
Girl Crazy. (NY) *Telegram* 15 Oct.
1930.

The reviewer called the show "one of the
few diverting entertainments of the new season."

B50   Boltinoff, Murray. "Theatrical
Sideshow: From Astoria to the Al-
vin." Unidentified clipping dated
Dec. 1934, Yale University Library
Archives, Porter Collection.

B51   Bordman, Gerald. *American Musical*
Comedy. New York: Oxford University

Press, 1982. pp. 463, 470, 471, 480, 490, 491, 499, 514, 518, 522, 533, 534, 543, 552, 553, 574, 602, 611, 612, 634, 642, 649, 678

B52   Botto, Louis. *At This Theatre: An Informal History of New York's Legitimate Theatres.* New York: Dodd, Mead, 1984. pp. 48, 129, 147, 148, 155

B53   Brooks, Tim and Earle Marsh. *The Complete Directory to Prime Time Network Television Shows 1946-Present.* New York: Ballantine Books, 1979. pp. 117, 127, 620

B54   Brown, John Mason. *Broadway in Review.* New York: W. W. Norton, 1940; rept. Freeport, NY: Books for Libraries Press, 1969. pp. 242-247

B55   ------------------. *"Du Barry Was a Lady* with Miss Merman and Mr. Lahr." Rev. of *Du Barry Was a Lady. New York Post* 7 Dec. 1939.

"Miss Merman sweeps through the evening with that bright-eyed, shining vitality which is always such as captivating feature of her playing and her singing. She needs no vitamins; she has plenty to spare. Her throat houses as beguiling a calliope as Broadway knows. The Midas touch is upon her tonsils because she can turn brass into gold. She can do more than that. She can keep it brass. No one can match her in putting a song across, in trumpeting its lyrics, in personifying its rhythms. . . ."

B56   ------------------. "La Merman." *Saturday Review* 29 (15 June 1946): 30-32.

B57   ----------------. "The Play." Rev.
of *Anything Goes.* *New York Post*
22 Nov. 1934.

"Miss Merman once again demonstrated how rare and captivating is her talent. . . . she brings her all-conquering vitality to both her acting and singing. . . ."

B58   ----------------. "Seeing Things."
Rev. of *Annie Get Your Gun.* *Saturday Review* 29 (May 1946).

"Even before the atomic bomb, there was Ethel Merman. . . . Has 'show biz' a symbol? She is it. What the Goddess of Liberty is to the harbor, Miss Merman is to Tin Pan Alley. . . . Miss Merman IS Broadway."

B59   ----------------. "Seeing More
Things." *Saturday Review* 29 (15 June 1946): 30-32.

B60   ----------------. "Two on the
Aisle." Rev. of *Red, Hot, and Blue!* *New York Post* 4 Nov. 1936.

After decrying the quality of Porter's songs, Brown commends Merman: "But it is Miss Merman's unique gift to sing every song that comes her way, so that while she is singing it seems good. . . . She is a zestful comedian, gay, likable, and expert. And as a projector of jazz she is unrivaled in our theatre."

B61   ----------------. "Two on the
Aisle." Rev. of *Take a Chance.* *New York Post* 28 Nov. 1932.

Merman "is once again making clear how rare is the contribution she has to make to the lilting world of rhymed passion that is known as musical comedy." Brown adds, "She knows what she is about and is able to do it.

More than that, she does it so that there is no withstanding it."

B62   ----------------. "With the Most-es' on the Ball." Rev. of *Call Me Madam*. *Saturday Review* 33 (28 Oct. 1950): 42-44.

The show is "a decided 'must' because of the overpowering fact that Ethel Merman is in it. . . . To refer to our planet as plundered when Miss Merman can be counted among its un-exhausted resources is to make a travesty of science. . . . Every line she reads, every song she sings, is as illuminated as the most dazzling of Times Square's electric signs."

B63   Brown, Sydney. "After 40 Years, 14 Musicals, She's Still Belting out the Songs." *Richmond (VA) News-Leader* 2 May 1980: A15.

B64   Bryan, George B. "Ethel Merman." *Notable Women in the American Theatre: A Biographical Dictionary*. Ed. Alice M. Robinson, Vera Mowry Roberts, and Milly S. Barranger. (Westport, CT: Greenwood Press, 1989): 631-634.

Thanks to agent Robert Gardiner, Merman read and approved this essay before its publication.

B65   Burrows, Abe. *Honest Abe: Is There Really No Business Like Show Business?* Boston: Little, Brown and Co., 1980. pp. 40, 209, 225, 280, 281-282, 283

B66   Bustard, C. A. "Miss Merman at Mosque." *Richmond (VA) Times-Dispatch* 3 May 1980: A8.

B67   Cahn, William. *Good Night, Mrs. Calabash: The Secret Life of Jimmy Durante.* New York: Duell, Sloan, and Pearce, 1963. pp. 126, 127, 129

B68   Cahoon, Herbert. "New Films." Rev. of *Call Me Madam.* *Library Journal* 78 (1 Apr. 1953): 588.

Merman "is a constant fascination in action and in song. . . . it is another personal triumph for Ethel Merman."

B69   Caldwell, Cy. "To See or not to See." Rev. of *We're not Dressing.* *New Outlook* 163 (June 1934): 45.

"Leon Errol and Ethel Merman are afforded only slight opportunities. . . ." The film is judged "not bad, not good."

B70   "Call Me Madam." Rev. of *Call Me Madam.* *Cue* 30 Sept. 1950.

B71   "Call Me Merman." Rev. of *Call Me Madam.* *Theatre Arts* 34 (Nov. 1950): 16-17.

B72   Calta, Louis. "Ethel Merman Agrees to Take Hello, Dolly! Lead for Three Months." *New York Times* 10 Mar. 1970: A52, 2-3.

B73   ------------. "Ethel Merman to Tour." *New York Times* 3 Mar. 1961: A17, 4.

B74   Carroll, Diahann and Ross Firestone. *Diahann: An Autobigraphy.* Boston: Little, Brown and Co., 1986. pp. 27, 39

Carroll observes that Merman's performance as Annie Oakley inspired her to be an actress. Years later, Carroll's singing coach advised her to learn how to deliver high notes by analyzing Merman's vocal technique.

B75   "'Chance,' $30,000 Looks B'way Smash." *Variety* 29 Nov. 1932: A49, 1.

B76   Chapman, John. "Miss Merman Has Her Best Role in *Gypsy*, a Real Life Musical." Rev. of *Gypsy*. (NY) *Daily News* 22 May 1959 in *New York Theatre Critics' Reviews* 1959: 302.

"... best of all is the story of Life with Mama and the way Miss Merman plays it."

B77   Chotzinoff, Samuel. *Toscanini: An Intimate Memoir*. New York: Alfred A. Knopf, 1956. p. 45

Chotzinoff writes of the conductor's delight in Merman's performance in *Panama Hattie*. Toscanini "laughed extravagantly at Miss Merman's down-to-earth deportment and admired her lung power."

B78   "Cinema: New Pictures: The Big Broadcast of 1936." Rev. of *The Big Broadcast of 1936*. *Time* 26 (23 Sept. 1935): 45-46.

"... the most enjoyable [moments] are those in which. ... Ethel Merman cavorts with a chorus of elephants to a tune called *It's the Animal in Me*."

B79   "Cinema: New Pictures: Anything Goes." Review of *Anything Goes*. *Time* 27 (3 Feb. 1936): 57.

This review contains no evaluation of Merman's performance.

B80   "Cinema: New Pictures: Strike Me Pink." Rev. of *Strike Me Pink*. *Time* 27 (27 Jan. 1936): 47, 1.

According to the reviewer, this is a better than usual Eddie Cantor film, thanks to Merman's presence.

B81   "Cinema: New Pictures: Happy Landing." Rev. of *Happy Landing*. *Time* 31 (31 Jan. 1938): 35.

"Ethel Merman sings with her usual lid-off verve like a hotcha stenographer at a house party, and skates a little bit."

B82   "Cinema: New Pictures: Alexander's Ragtime Band." Rev. of *Alexander's Ragtime Band*. *Time* 32 (15 Aug. 1938): 35.

B83   "Cinema: New Pictures: Straight, Place, and Show." Rev. of *Straight, Place, and Show*. *Time* 32 (3 Oct. 1938): 36.

This reviewer thinks the story hampered the entertainment value of the specialty acts. The "fable [i. e. the plot]. . . survives principally as the excuse for two songs by Ethel Merman. . . ."

B84   "Cinema: New Pictures: Stage Door Canteen." Rev. of *Stage Door Canteen*. *Time* 41 (14 June 1943): 94.

B85   Clurman, Harold. "Ethel Merman." Rev. of *Call Me Madam*. *New Republic* 123 (6 Nov. 1950): 23.

Clurman calls Merman "Broadway's only female tenor."

B86   Coe, Richard L. "The Merm Has Become Annie." Rev. of *Annie Get Your
Gun. Washington Post* 1 June 1966.

Merman's "voice is clear, strong and assured as Steuben glass. . . . Her precise,
unmistakable diction is sharp as ever and you
think to yourself that maybe one reason lyrics
have become so trivial is that few take the
trouble to utter them."

B87   Coleman, Emily R. *The Complete Judy
Garland.* New York: Harper and Row,
1990. pp. 305, 306, 327, 359, 362,
375, 381, 401

B88   Coleman, Robert. "Girl Crazy Sure
Gershwin Triumph." Rev. of *Girl
Crazy. New York Times* 15 Oct.
1930: 27, 1.

B89   ----------------. "Gypsy a Dynamic
Musical." Rev. of *Gypsy.* (NY) *Daily
Mirror* 22 May 1959 in *New York
Theatre Critics' Reviews* 1959: 300.

B90   Colonial, Elinor Hughes. "The Theatre." Rev. of *Red, Hot, and Blue!
Boston Herald* 8 Oct. 1936.

B91   Corkery, Richard. "Merm Lights up
the Hall." Rev. of Carnegie Hall
Concert. (NY) *Daily News* 4 May
1982.

"The lady. . . IS the American musical
theatre. . . ."

B92   *Creative America.* Ed. Jerry Mason.
Washington, DC: National Cultural
Center, 1962. p. 40
The book includes Dennis Stock's very
unflattering picture of Merman in *Call Me
Madam.*

B93   Crichton, Kyle. "Singing Merman."
                 Collier's 95 (16 Feb. 1935): 15,
                 50.

B94   Crosby, Bing and Pete Martin. *Call
                 Me Lucky*. New York: Simon and
                 Schuster, 1953. p. 227

    Crosby concludes that Mary Martin's per-
formance in *South Pacific* and Merman's in *Annie Get Your Gun* "are in a photo-finish for
the greatest I've ever watched on the musical-
comedy stage."

B95   Crowther, Bosley. "New Angles on an
                 Old Smoothie." *New York Times* 1
                 May 1938: J3, 1-3.

B96   Dale, George B. Jacket notes. *Gyp-
                 sy*. Columbia Records OL 5420, OS
                 2017, 1959.

B97   Danzig, Fred. "Sound Barrier Broken
                 by Ethel Merman." *Owensboro (KY)
                 Messenger-Inquirer* 25 Nov. 1959:
                 n. p.

    This Ford Startime TV special, broadcast
on 24 Nov. 1959, was notable for the twenty-
odd songs sung by Merman, but the reviewer was
justifiably disturbed by the decision to em-
ploy pre-recorded vocal tracks.

B98   Davy, C. Review of *Kid Millions*.
                 Spectator 154 (1 Feb. 1935): 162.

B99   De Long, Thomas A. *Pops: Paul
                 Whiteman, King of Jazz*. Piscataway,
                 NJ: New Century Publishers, 1983.
                 pp. 228, 277

B100   Dennis, L. "Ethel Merman: Queen of
                 Broadway." *Reader's Digest* 98
                 (June 1971): 112-116.

B101   Dienstfrey, Sherri R. "Ethel Merman: Queen of Musical Comedy." Diss. Kent State U, 1986.

The most useful facet of this dissertation is its utilization of interviews with Jerry Herman, Irving Katz, Robert Levitt, Jr., and Benay Venuta. The author's correspondence with George Abbott, George Burns, Lee Davis, Betty Garrett, Arthur Laurents, and Benay Venuta also provides interesting perspectives.

B102   Dietz, Howard. *Dancing in the Dark with Howard Dietz*. New York: Quadrangle, 1974. pp. 27-273

Dietz contends that Merman's leaving the production of *Sadie Thompson* was because of Bob Levitt's meddling, particularly his rewriting of Dietz' lyrics.

B103   DiOrio, Al, Jr. *The Life and Hard Times of Judy Garland*. New Rochelle, NY: Arlington House, 1973. pp. 30, 81, 163

B104   "A 'Doll' with Rhythm: Ethel Merman." *New York Times* 7 Dec. 1956: A31, 1.

B105   Drutman, Irving. "Eternal Merman." *Theater*, 18 September 1966.

B106   Dunning, John. *Tune in Yesterday: The Ultimate Encyclopedia of Old-Time Radio 1925-1976*. Englewood Cliffs, NJ: Prentice-Hall, 1976. pp. 37, 66, 186-187, 346

B107   Eager, Helen. "Ethel Merman at Shubert in *Call Me Madam*. Rev. of *Call Me Madam*. *Boston Traveler* 20 Sept. 1950.

"A first night audience, hanging on the rafters at the Shubert, raised callouses on its hands in tribute to her inimitable delivery. . . . She does her customary wonderful things. . . . And always she is enormously funny."

B108   Edwards, Anne. *Judy Garland: A Biography*. New York: Simon and Schuster, 1974. p. 209

B109   --------------. *A Remarkable Woman: A Biography of Katherine Hepburn*. New York: William Morrow, 1985. pp. 178, 334, 350

B110   Eells, George. *Cole Porter: The Life That Late He Led*. New York: Berkley Medallion Books, 1967. pp. 121, 122, 171-174, 176, 177, 210, 212, 214, 216, 217, 223, 229, 230, 250, 294, 307, 323, 352, 353, 359

B111   Efron, Edith. "Doin' What Comes Natur'lly." *TV Guide* 18 Mar. 1967: 10-14.

Efron writes of Merman's previous career as well as her forthcoming appearance on NBC-TV's version of *Annie Get Your Gun*, aired on 19 Mar. 1967.

B112   Engel, Lehman. *The American Musical Theatre: A Consideration*. New York: Macmillan, 1975. p. 65

B113   "Entertainment: 'Broadcast.'" Rev. of *The Big Broadcast of 1936*. *Newsweek* 6 (21 Sept. 1935): 17.

B114   "Entertainment: Alexander's Ragtime Band." Rev. of *Alexander's Ragtime Band*. *Newsweek* 12 (1 Aug. 1938): 18-19.

Without evaluating Merman's performance, the reviewer dubs the film "outstanding movie making."

B115   "Entertainment: Canteenful   of Stars." Rev. of *Stage Door Canteen*. *Newsweek*   21   (21 June 1943):   100, 102.

B116   Ephron, Henry. *We Thought We Could Do Anything*. New York: W. W. Norton, 1977.

Ephron and his wife Phoebe were involved with   the   screenplay of *There's No Business Like Show Business*.

B117   "Ethel Changes Tune." 14 Aug. 1966: 5. An unidentified clipping in the author's collection.

The   popularity   of   the   revival   of *Annie Get Your Gun* persuaded Merman both to take the production on a four-to-six-week tour and to extend the return engagement in New York.

B118   "Ethel Merman." *Current Biography* (New   York: H.   W.   Wilson,   1941): 573-575; 1955: 412-414; 1984: 476.

B119   "Ethel Merman and Her Magic." Rev. of *Gypsy*.   *Newsweek*   48   (31 Dec. 1956): 35-38.

"[T]he   show   would   be   memorable   for   the emergence of Ethel Merman as one of the first ladies of the stage, with or without music."

B120   "Ethel Merman and Los Angeles Philharmonic." *Variety*   15 Aug.   1978: A13.

B121   "Ethel Merman at Pars." *Variety*   9 June 1931: A32, 5.

After the closing of *Girl Crazy*, Merman was booked into the Brooklyn and New York Paramount Theatres for the week of 19-26 June.

B122   [Entry deleted.]

B123   "Ethel Merman Deal Hinted." *New York Times* 15 Feb. 1949: A50, 7.

B124   "Ethel Merman Files Protest." *New York Times* 22 Aug. 1957: A22, 3.

B125   "Ethel Merman Gets Divorce." *New York Times* 11 June 1952: A36, 7.

B126   "Ethel Merman Honored." *New York Times* 7 Oct. 1970: A37, 1.

Merman received the Actors' Fund of America's commendation for outstanding service and generosity.

B127   "Ethel Merman Hosts Rally Outside French and Polyclinic Hospital, Which Has Cared for Actors and Actresses." *New York Times* 9 Oct. 1975: A45, 5.

B128   "Ethel Merman Married." *New York Times* 21 Dec. 1941: A42, 5.

B129   "Ethel Merman on First Tour with 'Gypsy.'" Unidentified clipping from a newspaper in Shreveport, LA, in the author's collection.

Although it made good newspaper copy to claim that *Gypsy* was Merman's first tour, the facts prove otherwise.

B130   "Ethel Merman, or Stenographer into Star." *New York Times* 19 Feb. 1939: I2, 2-5.

B131   "Ethel Merman Paying Al Siegal [sic], Who Made Her, $105 out of $1,950 Wkly." *Variety* 12 Nov. 1930: A47, 3.

B132   "Ethel Merman Plans to Wed Ernest Borgnine." *New York Times* 28 Dec. 1963: A12, 1.

B133   "Ethel Merman Records Broadway Hits on Disco Album." *Washington Post* 12 Apr. 1979, DC ed.: A8, 1.

B134   "Ethel Merman Recuperating after Brain Surgery." *Washington Post* 16 Apr. 1983: C3, 1.

B135   "Ethel Merman Says Her Favorite Singing Partner Is Jack Klugman." *New York Times* 21 Sept. 1974: A15, 4.

B136   "Ethel Merman Seeks Divorce." *New York Times* 9 June 1952: A18, 6.

B137   "Ethel Merman Set with Jessel for N. Y. Par." *Variety* 24 Apr. 1934: A49, 1.

This vaudeville appearance is slated to open on 27 April at the Paramount Theatre.

B138   "Ethel Merman Subpoenaed." *New York Times* 2 Apr. 1958: A36, 1.

B139   "Ethel Merman to Ask Divorce." *New York Times* 15 Nov. 1960: A47, 3.

B140   "Ethel Merman to Be Honored Guest." *New York Times* 13 Dec. 1940: A29, 5.

Merman was the featured guest at a party given by the American Theatre Wing in aid of the British War Relief Society. Proceeds went to purchasing mobile kitchens for victims of the blitz.

B141   "Ethel Merman Undergoes Brain Surgery at Roosevelt Hospital." *Washington Post* 15 Apr. 1983: C2, 3.

B142   "Ethel Merman Wed to Robert F. Six in March." *New York Times* 7 June 1953: A80, 5.

B143   "Ethel Merman Will Get Barter Theatre Award." *New York Times* 27 May 1957: A26, 2.

B144   "Ethel Merman Wins Divorce." *New York Times* 19 Nov. 1964: A48, 8.

B145   "Ethel Merman's Daughter Is Found Dead in Colorado." *New York Times* 24 Aug. 1967: A37, 3.

B146   "Ethel Merman's 'Kiki'." *Variety* 25 Feb. 1931: A55, 4.

It is rumored that the Picard-Belasco play *Kiki* (1921) is to be made into a musical with Merman in the Lenore Ulric role. To be called *Singin' the Blues*, it is to be rehearsed in New York and opened in Atlantic City.

B147   "Ethel Merman's Mother Mrs. Agnes G. Zimmermann Dies on Jan. 14 at Age of 90." *New York Times* 15 Jan. 1974: A40, 3.

B148   Ewen, David. *All the Years of American Popular Music.* Englewood Cliffs, NJ: Prentice-Hall, 1977. pp. 339, 358, 364, 374, 375, 394, 417, 434, 440, 487-488, 513, 602, 604

B149   ------------. *Complete Book of the American Musical Theatre*. New York: Holt, Rinehart and Winston, 1965. pp. 29, 30, 31, 32, 49, 65, 111, 213, 215, 216, 217, 218, 219, 332, 378, 383

B150   ------------. *A Journey to Greatness: The Life and Music of George Gershwin*. New York: Henry Holt, 1956. 218-220, 307, 352, 353, 354

B151   ------------. *The Story of America's Musical Theatre*. Philadelphia: Chilton Co., 1961. pp. 118-120, 137, 139, 157, 200, 201, 217, 218

B152   Fairweather, D. Rev. of *Alexander's Ragtime Band*. *Theatre World* 30 (Nov. 1938): 230.

B153   Fairweather, Virginia. *Olivier: An Informal Portrait* [English title: *Cry God for Larry*]. New York: Coward-McCann, 1969. pp. 126, 127, 131

Fairweather relates an amusing anecdote about her encounter with Merman in Moscow.

B154   Faith, William R. *Bob Hope: A Life in Comedy*. New York: G. P. Putnam's Sons, 1982. pp. 19, 96, 103-106, 109, 363

B155   Farber, Manny. "When the Pie War Opened." Rev. of *Stage Door Canteen*. *New Republic* 109 (26 July 1943): 110.

Although she has little to do in the film, in the song "Marching through Berlin," Merman "swells out into something that is the best part of joy, getting full bounty from the worst lyric of the war."

B156   Ferguson, Otis. "The Great Dur-ante." Rev. of *Stars in Your Eyes*. *New Republic* 98 (1 Mar. 1939): 102-103.

B157   Ferretti, Fred. "Ethel Merman Belts out Songs on Concert Cir-cuit." *New York Times* 13 Mar. 1981: C3, 1-3.

B158   "Film House Reviews: Paramount, New York." *Variety* 23 June 1931: A39, 1.

Merman received a weekly salary of $2,750 for singing three songs, including "I Got Rhy-thm." She was good, and her leaving would hurt the rest of the show.

B159   "Filming of 'Chance' Set?" *Variety* 13 June 1933: A45, 5.

The producers of *Take a Chance* have de-cided to film the show with Merman as the only representative of the original cast. [The film was made (1933), but Lillian Roth played Merman's role.]

B160   Finch, Christopher. *Rainbow: The Stormy Life of Judy Garland*. New York: Grosset and Dunlap, 1975. pp. 73, 165

B161   "$500 a Side vs 3c Per for Merman on Discs." *Variety* 27 Sept. 1932: A59, 4.

Merman's 16-disc recording deal with RCA-Victor is discussed.

B162   Fowler, Gene.   *Schnozzola: The Story of Jimmy Durante*. New York: Viking Press, 1951. pp. 135, 200, 201, 211

Fowler claims that Durante's partner, Lou Clayton, changed the actress' name from Zimmerman [sic] to Merman. Merman's recollection (**B298**, p. 54) is quite different.

B163   Frank, Gerold. *Judy*. New York: Harper and Row, 1975. pp. 63, 74, 94, 96, 247, 299, 348, 422, 456, 457, 570

B164   Freedland, Michael. *Irving Berlin*. New York: Stein and Day, 1974. pp. 46, 133, 135, 170-171, 172, 185, 191, 194, 197, 207-208

B165   Funke, Lewis.   "Merman--Hello, Dolly's! Lucky 7th." *New York Times* 30 Mar. 1970: A52, 1-4.

B166   Gabriel, Gilbert. "Anything Goes." Rev. of *Anything Goes*. *American* Nov. 1934.

This reviewer thought Merman "a wizardress, I wouldn't dare say a witch putting most of those lyrics across. What she does with the provocative jingles of the piece 'Anything Goes' is anybody's funeral."

B167   Garland, Robert. "Annie Get Your Gun." Rev. of *Annie Get Your Gun*. (NY) *Journal-American* 17 May 1946.

"She's no longer Miss Merman acting like Ethel Merman. She's Miss Merman acting like Annie Oakley."

B168   ---------------. "Cast and Miscast: A High and Mighty Audience Applauds

George White's Scandals at the
Apollo." Rev. of *George White's
Scandals*. (NY) *Journal-American*
Sept. 1931.

B169   ---------------. "Ethel Merman's
Big, Good Natured Show." Rev. of
Call Me Madam. (NY) *Journal-
American* 13 Oct. 1950 in *New York
Theatre Critics' Reviews* 1950: 244.

The piece "is Ethel Merman's show from
start to finish. It is her show when she is on
the stage. It is her show when she is off. It
is her show when Paul Lukas is being charming.
It is her show when Russell Nype is being
good. . . . But as I have said, Call Me Madam
is Ethel Merman's. And this is how I like it!"

B170   ---------------. "Mr. Porter Shines
in Anything Goes." Rev. of *Anything
Goes*. (NY) *Journal-American* 22
Nov. 1934.

B171   Gavin, James. *Intimate Nights: The
Golden Age of New York Cabarets*.
New York: Grove Weidenfeld, 1991.
pp. 31, 63, 138, 141, 142-143, 147,
198, 213, 243, 304, 324, 325, 333

Although Merman's cabaret appearances an-
tedated and postdated Gavin's period, he re-
peats several, often unflattering anecdotes
about her as a customer.

B172   Geduld, Harry M. "Clipped Wings."
Rev. of *Airplane!* *Humanist* 41, 6
(Nov.-Dec. 1980): 45-46.

B173   "Gershwin Concert Has Record
Crowd." *New York Times* 10 Aug.
1937: A22, 4.

20,223 people assembled in Lewisohn Stadium to pay tribute to the composer. ". . . Miss Ethel Merman. . . appeared in white, gold, and fur before a specially placed purplish spotlight to sing, in a voice and style that need no special description, 'The Man I Love,' 'They Can't Take That Away from Me,' and 'I Got Rhythm.' Miss Merman, received with great demonstration, repeated 'I Got Rhythm' to the great joy of the audience."

B174   Gibbs, Wolcott. "Ethel Is Back." *New Yorker* 32 (22 Dec. 1956): 54.

B175   --------------. "Our Miss Merman." Rev. of *Something for the Boys*. *New Yorker* 18 (16 Jan. 1943): 32.

Merman's "hair-raising voice" is superbly adapted to making a bad song sound good.

B176   --------------. "Queen of Musical Comedy." *Life* 21 (8 July 1946): 84-88.

B177   --------------. "A Rose for Miss Merman." Rev. of *Call Me Madam*. *New Yorker* 26 (21 Oct. 1950): 55.

"The reasons for her appeal are unfathomable. It is the perpetual riddle of genius."

B178   --------------.   "The Theatre: Ethel and Anton." Rev. of *Annie Get You Gun*. *New Yorker* 22 (25 May 1946): 42.

After observing that Merman "has the gift of suggesting a wide range of emotion without perceptibly altering her expression," Gibbs concludes that Merman is "a great deal more rewarding than Chekhov." *Uncle Vanya* was then being seen in New York.

B179   Gielgud, John. "Ethel Merman" in
         Double Exposure ed. by Roddy Mc-
         Dowall. New York: Delacorte Press,
         1966. pp. 148-149

    A full page photograph of Merman in her
apartment accompanies Gielgud's observations.
"The voice of Miss Merman, on radio or phono-
graph record, does not prepare one for the
artistry with which she uses it when one first
sees her on the stage. . . . one sighs with
satisfaction at the perfection of her technique and the apparent ease and skill with
which she can take such unquestionable command
of a huge audience."

B180   Gilbert,   Douglas.   "'Flowers?
         Where's   the   Body?'   asks   Ethel
         Merman,   'the   Gal   Who   Made   Cin-
         derella   Just   a   Sob   Story.'"   *New
         York World-Telegram*   24 Nov. 1934.

B181   Gilder, Rosamond. "Broadway in Re-
         view: Broadway Does Something for
         the Boys." Rev. of *Something for
         the Boys*. *Theatre Arts* 27 (March
         1943): 138-139.

    Merman acts "with a minumum of gesture
and a maximum of innuendo."

B182   ----------------.   "Broadway   in
         Review: Sweet Creatures of Bom-
         bast." Rev. of *Stars in Your Eyes*.
         Theatre Arts 23 (Apr. 1939): 242-
         243.

B183   ----------------.   "Broadway   in
         Review: Tragedy and Tinsel." Rev.
         of *Du Barry Was a Lady*. *Theatre
         Arts* 24 (Feb. 1940): 92-93.

B184   ----------------.   "Broadway   in
         Review: Fiddling While Rome Burns."

Rev. of *Panama Hattie*. *Theatre Arts* 25 (Jan. 1941): 12-13.

B185   Gill, Brendan. *Cole*. Ed. Robert Kimball. New York: Holt, Rinehart, and Winston, 1971. pp. xviii, 123, 126, 142, 144, 145, 146, 160, 161, 162, 163, 164, 175, 176, 190, 192, 193

All references except the first are to production photographs.

B186   Glover, William. "Ethel Merman IS Lucky 7 as Dolly! Nears a Record." Rev. of *Hello, Dolly! Philadelphia Inquirer* 17 May 1970.

Merman is "Broadway's one and only big brass band. . . ."

B187   ---------------. "Ethel Merman Turns Actress." *Louisville (KY) Courier-Journal* 21 June 1959: F1.

Glover reports Merman's desire to become a dramatic actress when she could no longer be a singer. This determination came after her success in *Gypsy*.

B188   ---------------. "Queens Reign on-- Newcomers Scarce on B'Way." *Evansville (IN) Courier*, 31 Dec. 1959: A22.

Merman, "who added acting ability to her renowned vocal prowess in 'Gypsy,'" is identified as a reigning queen.

B189   Goldman, William. *The Season: A Candid Look at Broadway*. New York: Bantam Books, 1970. pp. 14, 174

Although appreciative of Merman's work, Goldman deprecates her practice of "freezing" a performance. "This is her way of working, and no one works harder; still, after the opening, what you see is a Xerox of the original."

B190   Good, Paul. "The Belter." *New York Sunday News Magazine* 9 May 1982: A6-11.

B191   Gordon, Max and Lewis Funke. *Max Gordon Presents*. New York: Bernard Geis Associates, 1963. p. 262

B192   Gottfried, Martin. "Mary and Ethel Return the Magic to Broadway." Rev. of *Together on Broadway*. *New York Post* 21 May 1977: A32.

B193   ----------------. *A Theater Divided: The Postwar American Stage*. Boston: Little, Brown, 1967. pp. 45, 194-196

Gottfried discusses the potential professional dangers of becoming a favorite of the homosexual community. Merman, along with Judy Garland, Tallulah Bankhead, and others, is discussed in this context.

B194   Gould, Jack. "Ethel Merman Brings What Zest She Can to CBS Adaptation of Panama Hattie." Rev. of *Panama Hattie*. *New York Times* 12 Nov. 1954: A29, 3, 4.

Aside from Merman's numbers, the reviewer thought the telecast lifeless.

B195   ----------. "Television: 'Annie' on Tape." Rev. of *Annie Get Your Gun*. *New York Times* 20 Mar. 1967: A63, 4.

B196   ------------. "Television in Review: Song Magic." Rev. of *Anything Goes*. *New York Times* 3 Mar. 1954: A35, 2, 4.

B197   ------------.   "Television Review: Ethel Merman Offers an Hour of Song." Rev. of *Merman on Broadway*. *New York Times* 25 Nov. 1959: A59, 5.

B198   ------------. "TV: Profile of Mike Todd." *New York Times* 9 Sept. 1968: A93, 1.

Merman reminisced about Todd's temerity in telling Cole Porter how to write songs and her how to sing them.

B199   Grady, Billy. *The Irish Peacock: The Confessions of a Legendary Talent Agent*. New Rochelle, NY: Arlington House, 1972. pp. 7, 283

B200   Grauer, Bill, Jr. and Orrin Keep- news. Jacket notes, *On-Stage, Volume 1: Ethel Merman and Gertrude Niesen*, "X" Vault Originals, LVA-1004.

B201   Green, Abel. "Disc Reviews." *Variety* 30 Oct. 1934: A44, 2.

With accompaniment by Johnny Green, Merman's recordings of "An Earful of Music" and "You're a Builder Upper" are examples of "Miss Merman's modern manner. . . at its best. . . ."

B202   ------------. "Disc Reviews." *Variety* 18 Sept. 1935: A33, 4.

"The Lady in Red" and "It's the Animal in Me" are "distinguished by La Merman's usually vivid vocal style."

B203   ----------- and Joe Laurie, Jr. *Show Biz: From Vaude to Video*. New York: Henry Holt, 1951. pp. 503, 546-547, 562

B204   Green, Stanley. *The Great Clowns of Broadway*. New York: Oxford University Press, 1984. pp. 60, 61, 62, 63-64, 94, 95, 98, 103, 118, 119, 169

Although Merman is not one of the clowns of the title, some of her scenes with Jimmy Durante, Willie Howard, Bert Lahr, and Victor Moore are highlighted.

B205   --------------. Jacket notes. *Merman: Her Greatest*. Reprise R-6032.

B206   Gros. Rev. of *Lincoln Center Day*. *Variety* 26 Sept. 1963: A35, 1.

B207   --------------. *The World of Musical Comedy*. Cranbury: A. S. Barnes, 1960. pp. 100-101, 102, 111, 115, 134-135, 149, 167-168, 171, 173-175, 176, 192, 204, 284, 288-291; 2nd ed., 19--; 3rd ed., 1974.

B208   Guernsey, Otis L., Jr. *Broadway Song and Story: Playwrights/ Lyricists/Composers Discuss Their Hits*. New York: Dodd, Mead, 1985. pp. 55, 56, 60, 61, 62, 67, 68, 69, 70, 197, 205, 286, 288, 393

B209   "Gypsy." Rev. of *Gypsy*. *Coronet* 46 (Oct. 1959): 12.

The reviewer apparently did not appreci-
ate Merman's earlier efforts, but praises her
performance as Rose, "a robust, vital characterization," and her rendition of "Rose's
Turn," "an electrifying piece of bravura."

B210   "'Gypsy': A Memoir with Music (for
            G String)." Rev. of *Gypsy*. *Theatre
            Arts* 43 (May 1959): 18-20.

B211   "'Gypsy' Could Do $81,000 a Week."
            Variety 15 Apr. 1959: A149, 4.

B212   "Gypsy Fortune: In Black Pronto,
            Recoups $435,981 Net in 21 Weeks."
            Variety 14 Oct. 1959: A1, 1; A63,
            4.

B213   "'Gypsy' Runaway $82,992."   *Life*
            47 (27 July 1959): 63-64.

B214   Hall, Mordaunt. "The Screen." Rev.
            of *We're not Dressing*. *New York
            Times* 26 Apr. 1934: A27, 2.

B215   Hammond, Percy. "The Best of the
            Scandals." Rev. of *George White's
            Scandals*. *New York Herald-Tribune*
            Sept. 1931.

B216   --------------. "The Theatre." Rev.
            of *Anything Goes*. *New York Herald-
            Tribune* 22 Nov. 1934.

"Miss Merman, that rough and subtle scar-
let warbler, sings and acts a Broadway floor-
show prima donna laughably and with sincer-
ity."

B217   --------------. "The Theatre." Rev.
            of *Take a Chance*. *New York Herald-
            Tribune* 28 Nov. 1932.

B218   Harakas, Henry.   "Ethel Still a
             Showstopper." *Biography News* 2
             (Jan. 1975): 150.

B219   Hartung, Philip.   "Come on and
             Hear." Rev. of *Alexander's Ragtime
             Band*. *Commonweal* 28 (12 Aug.
             1938): 411.

B220   ---------------. "The Stage and
             Screen." Rev. of *Stage Door Can-
             teen*. *Commonweal* 38 (2 July
             1943): 275-276.

Although Merman sings in her "best manner," the film is too diverse to be successful.

B221   ---------------. "The Screen: Mad
             Madam Merman." Rev. of *It's a Mad,
             Mad, Mad, Mad World*. *Commonweal*
             57 (3 Apr. 1953): 649.

Merman "may be flashy, noisy, and even
naively vulgar, but her zest for life is un-
quenchable." The film is "among the year's
best movies."

B222   ---------------. "The Screen:
             There's No Schmaltz Like Show
             Schmaltz." Rev. of *There's No
             Business Like Show Business*.
             Commonweal 61 (24 Dec. 1954): 334.

"Ethel Merman and Dan Dailey are so de-
lightful. . . and so warm and parently. . .
that most of the picture takes on a friendly
and fun-loving glow."

B223   ---------------. "The Screen:
             Though This Be Madness." Rev. of
             It's a Mad, Mad, Mad, Mad World.
             Commonweal 79 (29 Nov. 1963):
             284.

"Merman's raucous harridan act, funny at first, becomes monotonous. . . ."

B224   Hatch, Robert. "Theatre." Rev. of
            Happy Hunting. *Nation* 188 (6 June
            1959): 521-522.

B225   Hawkins, William. "A Bull's Eye for
            Ethel Merman." Rev. of *Annie Get
            Your Gun*. N. P. 17 May 1946, un-
            identified clipping in the Museum
            of the City of New York, Theatre
            Collection.

Merman "sings with all the old lusty vitality, but more color in her voice. She acts
her comedy broadly but straight, with the deft
timing one expects of her. . . . Merman is
bright as a whip, sure as her shooting and
generously the foremost lady clown of her
time."

B226   Hay, Peter. *Theatrical Anecdotes*.
            New York: Oxford University Press,
            1987. pp. 44, 55-56

In addition to the oft-repeated assertion
of Merman's lack of stage fright, Hay relates
an interesting anecdote about her uneasy retirement when married to Robert Six.

B227   "Hearing at Equity on Actor Can-
            celed." *New York Times* 4 Jan.
            1958: A8, 3.

B228   Helburn, Theresa. *A Wayward Quest*.
            Boston: Little, Brown and Co.,
            1960. p. 217

Helburn says she tried to interest Richard Rodgers and Lorenz Hart in creating a musical version of Aristophanes' *Lysistrata* as a
vehicle for Merman.

B229 Henderson, Mary C. *Theater in America: 200 Years of Plays, Players, and Productions*. New York: Harry N. Abrams, 1986. pp. 132, 180, 182, 183

B230 Hewes, Henry. "Broadway Postscript." Rev. of *Happy Hunting*. *Saturday Review* 39 (29 Dec. 1956): 25.

B231 Hirschhorn, Clive. *The Hollywood Musical*. NY: Crown Publishing Co., 1981. pp. 62, 79, 87, 96, 106, 112, 113, 132, 145, 151, 152, 212, 221, 226, 271, 314, 334, 345, 355, 376

B232 Holden, Anthony. *Laurence Olivier: A Biography*. New York: Atheneum, 1988. p. 269

B233 Holden, Stephen. "Cabaret." Rev. of *Call Me Ethel*, by Rita McKenzie and Christopher Powich. *New York Times* 29 Jan. 1988: C25, 1-2.

Call Me Ethel is a one-woman show based on Merman's life.

B234 Hope, Bob and Pete Martin. *Have Tux, Will Travel*. New York: Simon and Schuster, 1954. pp. 121-123, 127

B235 "Hostess with the Mostes'." *Life* 29 (18 Sept. 1950): 92.

B236 Hurren, Kenneth A. "Ethel Merman." *What's on in London* 28 Feb. 1964: 23.

In this article advertising Merman's concert at London's Talk of the Town, the reviewer admits his distaste for the conceit evident in her first autobiography (**B308**), but he "can see now that for her to pretend to any modesty about her vocal gifts would be wanton affectation."

B237   "Husband Sues Ethel Merman." *New York Times* 7 Aug. 1941: A14, 3.

B238   Hutchinson, David. Jacket notes, *Red, Hot, and Blue! and Stars in Your Eyes*. AEI, 1984.

B239   Isaacs, Edith J. R. "Broadway in Review." Rev. of *Anything Goes*. *Theatre Arts* 19 (Jan. 1935): 19.

B240   Israel, Lee. *Miss Tallulah Bankhead*. New York: Dell, 1972. pp. 265, 275

B241   Jablonski, Edward and Lawrence D. Stewart. *The Gershwin Years*. Garden City, NY: Doubleday and Co., 1973. pp. 158, 321, 348, 392

B242   ------------------. *Gershwin*. Garden City, NY: Doubleday and Co., 1987. pp. 201, 202, 368

B243   Jackson, Arthur. *The Best Musicals from Show Boat to A Chorus Line*. New York: Crown Publishers, 1977.

B244   Jessel, George and John Austin. *The World I Lived In*. Chicago: Henry Regnery, 1975. p. 196

"The best of the comics. . . Ethel Merman and Martha Raye on the distaff side."

B245   Kahn. Rev. of *The Ethel Merman Show*. *Variety* 3 Aug. 1949: A26, 1.

"It seemed a bright idea to star her in a first-person situational comedy airer. The execution is something else again. Chalk this up as a missout."

B246   Kass, Robert. "Film and Television." Rev. of *Call Me Madam*. *Catholic World* 177 (May 1953): 142.

"Ethel Merman's explosive personality has at last found a movie role expansive enough to allow full range to her multiple talents. . . ." The film is the "freshest, funniest, fastest musical Hollywood has produced in years."

B247   Kauffmann, Stanley. "Films: Funny Ha-Ha and Funny Peculiar." Rev. of *It's a Mad, Mad, Mad, Mad World*. *New Republic* 149 (16 Nov. 1963): 26-27.

The reviewer writes of Merman's "bad acting and 'dead-eyes'--which were secondary when she was a brassy song-belter--are now all she has left."

B248   Keating, John. "A Marathon Named Merman." *Theatre Arts* 49, 9 (Sept. 1960): 62-65, 72-75.

B249   Kendall, Alan. *George Gershwin*. New York: Universe Books, 1987. pp. 103-104, 128

B250   Kerr, Walter. "Gypsy." Rev. of *Gypsy*. (NY) *Herald-Tribune* 22 May 1959, in *New York Theatre Critics' Reviews* 1959: 301.

Rose is "in short, a brassy, brazen witch on a mortgaged broom-stick, a steamroller with

cleats, the very mastodon of all stage moth-
ers. And you love her. . . ."

B251   ------------. *Journey to the Center
of the Theatre.* New York: Alfred A.
Knopf, 1979. pp. 58, 59, 246-247,
248, 252, 261-262

B252   ------------. "Merman: A Kid Who
Wins All the Marbles." Rev. of
Hello, Dolly! *New York Times* 12
Apr. 1970: B1, 1; B3, 3-6.

"My God, what a woman she is. Her comic
sense is every bit as authoritative, as high-
handed really, as her singing voice. . . missing Merman in the role would be like waiting
until Burbage had left Hamlet or Bernhardt had
called it quits with Camille. You've got to
come when the siren calls."

B253   ------------. "The Stage." Rev. of
Call Me Madam. *Commonweal* 53 (3
Nov. 1950): 94-95.

Kerr praises Merman's performance but
censures her "ungenerous deportment in not
sharing the 'You're Just in Love' bows with
Mr. Nype."

B254   Kimball, Robert and Alfred Simon.
The Gershwins. New York: Atheneum,
1973.

B255   Kislan, Richard. *The Musical--A
Look at the American Musical The-
atre.* Englewood Cliffs, NJ: Prentice-Hall, 1980. pp. 146, 218

Kislan makes the point that Jule Styne
tailored Rose's songs in *Gypsy* to Merman's
preference and in the same paragraph inter-
estingly observes, ". . .special material
carries with it a built-in liability. A show

whose elements are built to a star's unique gifts may not survive the star's departure."

B256   Kolodin, Irving. "Life with Madam." Rev. of *Call Me Madam*. *Saturday Review* 33 (30 Sept. 1950): 49-50.

B257   Kreuger, Miles.   Jacket notes. *Ethel Merman--Lyda Roberti--Mae West*.   Columbia Records, CL2751, 1967.

B258   Krutch, Joseph Wood. "Drama." Rev. of *Red, Hot, and Blue!*   *Nation* 143 (14 Nov. 1936): 585.

"Merman reigns supreme as the exponent of a style she seems to have invented. No one else that I have ever heard seems to me to have achieved a combination of superficial blatancy with subtle undercurrents of nuance and satire so perfectly the expression of the spirit of jazz."

B259   ------------------. "Drama." Rev. of *Stars in Your Eyes*. *Nation* 148 (25 Feb. 1939): 245.

B260   ------------------.   "Drama: Christmas Suggestions." Rev. of *Du Barry Was a Lady*. *Nation* 149 (23 Dec. 1939): 716.

B261   Lahr, John. *Notes on a Cowardly Lion*. New York: Ballantine Books, 1969. pp. 130, 143, 235-242

B262   Langner, Lawrence. *The Magic Curtain*. New York: E. P. Dutton, 1951. p. 368

Langner discusses the Theatre Guild's idea of starring Merman in Aristophanes' *Lysistrata*.

B263   Laufe, Abe. *Broadway's Greatest Musicals*. New York: Grossman, 1976. pp. 34-36, 38-40, 43, 91-97, 139-143, 240-246, 323, 386

B264   Laurie, Joe, Jr. *Vaudeville: From the Honky-Tonks to the Palace*. New York: Henry Holt, 1953.   pp. 54, 495

Laurie's discussion of attempts to keep the Palace Theatre open by booking superstars in week-long engagements gives a useful footnote to Merman's career.

B265   Lerman, Leo.   "At the Theatre." Rev. of *Gypsy*. *Dance Magazine* 33 (July 1959): 12-13.

B266   "Les Ambassadeurs." Rev. of Clayton, Jackson, and Durante. *Variety* 9 Oct. 1929: A80, 2.

Merman is merely listed as part of the act, which also included Isabella Dwan and Minnie Tradgette.

B267   Lesley, Cole. *Remembered Laughter: The Life of Noël Coward*. New York: Alfred A. Knopf, 1976. pp. 183, 344, 381

B268   Levy, Newman.   "Drama: Three Shows with Music."   Rev. of *Girl Crazy*. *Nation* 131 (29 Oct. 1930): 479-80.

". . . and in Ethel Merman the Gershwins have a worthy interpreter of their songs."

B269   Lewis, Theophilus. "Theatre."   Rev. of *Annie Get Your Gun*.   *America* 114 (25 June 1966): 882.

Although he writes of "Merman's perfectionist portrayal of Annie," one suspects that Lewis' critical standards are more religious than artistic.

B270 ------------------. "Theatre." Rev. of *Gypsy*. *America* 101 (13 June 1959): 438.

The Merman voice in this review, strangely enough, is called "sultry."

B271 "Life and Times of Ethel Merman." *Time* 36 (28 Oct. 1940): 65-67.

B272 Little, Stuart and Arthur Cantor. *The Playmakers*. New York: W. W. Norton, 1970. pp. 49, 196, 212, 245

B273 Litton, Glenn and Cecil Smith. *Musical Comedy in America*. New York: Theatre Arts Books, 1981. pp. 49, 152-153, 155, 172, 178-179, 182, 185-186, 214, 231-232, 259, 272, 314

B274 Lockridge, Richard. "Du Barry Was a Lady with Ethel Merman Opens at the 46th Street." Rev. of *Du Barry Was a Lady*. *New York Sun* 7 Dec. 1939.

B275 ------------------. "The New Play." Rev. of *Red, Hot, and Blue!* *New York Sun* 31 Oct. 1936.

"Miss Merman is Miss Merman, always quite enough for your deponent. . . . Mr. Porter, who failed, for once, to give her the songs she should have had and made her waste her unrivaled technic [sic] and artful rhythm on his second best tunes."

B276   ------------------. "The New Play."
Rev. of *Stars in Your Eyes*. *New
York Sun* 10 Feb. 1939.

B277   ------------------. "The Stage in
Review." Rev. of *Take a Chance*. *New
York Sun* Nov. 1932.

Merman's performance of "Rise and Shine"
and "Eadie Was a Lady" was so electrifying
that it "halted proceedings."

B278   Logan, Joshua.   *Josh: My Up and
Down In and Out Life*. New York:
Delacorte Press, 1976.   pp. 137,
141-143, 215, 222-229, 244

B279   -------------. *Movie Stars, Real
People, and Me*. New York: Dela-
corte Press, 1978. pp. 76, 79-80,
235-236, 348

In November 1966 Merman sang before a
delighted Princess Margaret and her husband at
a party given by Logan. The director recalls
that during a performance of the revival of
Annie Get Your Gun Merman "found herself
looking directly at the naked buttocks of the
leading male dancer. Her reaction was such a
look of delighted surprise that it brought
equal delight from the audience."

B280   Lowry, Cynthia. "TV-Radio News." An
unidentified clipping in the au-
thor's collection.

Leland Hayward, producer of *The Gershwin
Years* for TV (aired 15 Jan. 1961), includes
Merman in his list of real stars among contem-
porary performers. She appeared on the show.

B281   Lynch, Richard C. "For the Record:
Ethel Merman." *Show Music*   6, 4
(Summer 1989): 35-39.

Lynch's excellent work on this article in two installments has been indispensable to the discography of this book.

B282   ---------------. "For the Record: Ethel Merman, Part 2." *Show Music* 7, 1 (Spring 1991): 54-57.

B283   Mander, Raymond and Joe Mitchenson. *Musical Comedy: A Story in Pictures*. New York: Taplinger, 1969.

B284   Maney, Richard. *Fanfare: The Confessions of a Press Agent*. New York: Harper and Row, 1957. pp. 11, 187, 237, 238, 270, 278

B285   Manning, M. "You Can't Tell Some People There Is No Santa Claus." *American Home* Dec. 1946: 26.

B286   Mantle, Burns. "Anything Goes, or Fun on the Ocean Wave." Rev. of *Anything Goes*. (NY) *Daily News* 22 Nov. 1934.

B287   ---------------. "George White's Scandals: First Cheers of the Season and Incident of Apollo Theatre Opening." Rev. of *George White's Scandals*. (NY) *Daily News* Sept. 1931.

The Merman voice is called "vibrant."

B288   ---------------. "Girl Crazy Added to Lay List." (NY) *Daily News* 16 Oct. 1930.

B289   ---------------. "Panama Hattie: Hot Number Fresh from the Canal." Rev. of *Panama Hattie*. (NY) *Daily News* 13 Oct. 1940.

B290   ------------.   "Red,   Hot,   and
             Blue!" Rev. of *Red, Hot, and Blue!*
             (NY) *Daily News* 13 Oct. 1936.

B291   ------------. "Take a Chance: A
             Lively Burlesque." Rev. of *Take a
             Chance.* (NY) *Daily News* 28 Nov.
             1932.

B292   Mantle,   Russet.   "The   Play   and
             Screen."   Rev. of *Strike Me Pink.*
             Commonweal 23 (31 Jan. 1936): 386.

"Decorative Ethel Merman, of radio and
Broadway, really is the main attraction in
song, performing in her best low-down blues
manner."

B293   Marks, Marcia. "Broadway." Rev. of
             Annie Get Your Gun. *Dance Magazine*
             40 (July 1966): 27, 59.

"Her voice is no longer sounding brass,
her figure has the amplitude of age, and she
moves, when she moves at all, like one of
those barrellike toys that bolt stiff-legged
down a ramp, but as the song says, "There's No
Business Like Show Business," and there's no
show business like Ethel Merman's. . . . If
Merman's voice no longer bellows, it's no
tinkling cymbal; it hits true and clear."

B294   Marshall, Margaret. "Drama." Rev.
             of *Call Me Madam.* *Nation* 171 (21
             Oct. 1950): 370.

B295   Martin, Mary. *My Heart Belongs.* New
             York: William Morrow, 1976. pp. 62-
             63, 145, 147, 149, 155-156, 198-
             201, 272, 313

B296   Marx, Arthur. *Red Skelton.* New
             York: E. P. Dutton, 1979. p. 103

Merman's name is mentioned once and ob-
liquely, which is surprising in view of Skelton's association with Merman on stage and
television.

B297   Marx, Samuel and Joyce Vanderveen.
         *Deadly Illusions: Jean Harlow and
         the Murder of Paul Bern.* New York:
         Random House, 1990. p. 29

Merman was considered for the starring
role in the film *Red-Headed Woman*, which made
a star of Jean Harlow.

B298   Mast, Gerald. *Can't Help Singin':
         The American Musical on Stage and
         Screen.* Woodstock, NY: Overlook
         Press, 1987. pp. 31, 42, 43, 71,
         188, 193, 194, 195, 196, 203, 227,
         229, 230, 294, 295, 318, 333, 340,
         350

B299   Mates, Julian. *America's Musical
         Stage: 200 Years of Musical
         Theatre.* Westport, CT: Greenwood
         Press, 1985. pp. 187, 194

B300   Maxwell, Elsa. "Elsa Maxwell's
         Party Line: Annie Get Your Gun."
         Rev. of *Annie Get Your Gun.* *New
         York Post* 8 Aug. 1946.

B301   McClain, John. "A Huge Night for
         Merman and Her Fans." Rev. of
         Gypsy. (NY) *Journal-American* 22 May
         1959, in *New York Theatre Critics'
         Reviews* 1959: 303.

B302   "Merman and Company Come to Town."
         Theatre Arts 41 (Feb. 1957): 72-
         76.

This article details the preproduction
ballyhoo of *Happy Hunting*.

B303   "Merman and Dietrich in London."
         Los Angeles Times 18 Sept. 1974:
         D22, 1.

B304   "Merman Leaving for H'wood; 'Goes'
         Sticks." *Variety*   29 May 1935:
         A53, 1.

B305   Merman, Ethel. "Ethel Merman's
         Favorite Stories about Her Rich and
         Famous Friends." *Star* 13 Mar. 1984:
         47.

    This article is a second installment of
anecdotes quoted from Merman's last autobiography (**B307**)

B306   --------------. "Her Work All Play
         to Ethel Merman." *New York Journal*
         21 Nov. 1936.

B307   ------------- and George Eells.
         Merman: An Autobiography. New York:
         Simon and Schuster, 1978.

B308   ------------ and Pete Martin. *Who
         Could Ask for Anything More?* Garden
         City, NY: Doubleday, 1955.

B309   ------------- and Pete Martin.
         "That's the Kind of Dame I Am:
         Excerpts from 'Doin' What Comes
         Natcherly.'" *Saturday Evening Post*
         227 (12 Feb. 1955): 17-19; (26 Feb.
         1955): 22-23; (5 Mar. 1955): 32-33;
         (12 Mar. 1955): 30+; 19 Mar. 1955):
         30+; (26 Mar. 1955): 36+.

    These articles comprise **B308**. Martin's
interview tapes are in the archives at the
University of Southern California.

B310   "Merman-Siegal [sic] Doubling,"
         Variety 8 Oct. 1930: A43, 2.

The team, while performing in *Girl Crazy*, is slated to open on 15 October at the Club Richman. As it happened, Siegel became ill and had to cancel the date. Merman barely escaped being restrained from appearing at the Casino in the Park.

B311   "Merman's Adventure: New NBC Radio Program." *Newsweek* 34 (15 Aug. 1949): 50.

B312   "Merman's Magic Enchants Britain." *New York Times* 2 Mar. 1964: A24, 2.

B313   Mesta, Perle and Robert Cahn. *Perle: My Story*. New York: Avon Books, 1960. pp. 8, 9, 141, 161

B314   Meyer, John. *Heartbreaker*. Garden City, NY: Doubleday, 1983. pp. 40, 101, 232

B315   Michael, Anthony. "Merman Still Mesmerizing 'Em." *Los Angeles Times* 3 Aug. 1977: D14, 1-2.

Merman has "the greatest singing voice in the nonoperatic musical theatre."

B316   Mielziner, Jo. *Designing for the Theatre: A Memoir and a Portfolio*. New York: Bramhall House, 1965.

B317   Milland, Ray. *Wide-Eyed in Babylon: An Autobiography*. New York: Ballantine Books, 1974. p. 178

B318   Millstein, Gilbert. "Madam Ambassador from and to Broadway." Rev. of *Call Me Madam*. *New York Times Magazine* 1 Oct. 1950: F24, F25, F73.

Merman "has the garish attraction of the honky tonk, of Coney Island and a merry-go-round. Why, damn it, she's a real, fleshly attractive personality. She's unique. She has a perfectly ingenious approach to things. She comes right to the point. She has that indefinable extra something which sends over waves into the people. It's hard to label. It's animal magnetism or something."

B319   Milton, Frank. *Name Dropping*. New York: E. P. Dutton, 1988. p. 88

Milton gives a firsthand account of Merman's concert at Carnegie Hall.

B320   Minnelli, Vincente and Hector Arce. *I Remember It Well*. Garden City, NY: Doubleday, 1974. p. 89

When Minnelli's career surged forward in 1937, someone suggested that he create a musical version of Euripides' *Medea* starring Merman.

B321   "Miss Merman to Rewed." *New York Times*   26 June 1964: A32, 3.

B322   Mordden, Ethan. *Better Foot Forward*. New York: Grossman, 1976. pp. xi, 72, 134-137, 149, 195, 236, 243, 268, 271, 272, 277-278, 292, 293, 306, 328

B323   --------------. *Broadway Babies: The People Who Made the American Musical*. New York: Oxford University Press, 1983.   5, 34, 67-68, 87, 114-120, 137, 161, 167, 181, 195, 199, 200, 201, 210, 213, 216, 217, 219-220, 221, 227, 232, 233, 238

B324   Morehouse, Ward. "Annie Get Your Gun Hit at the Imperial: Merman Overcomes Flimsy Book." Rev. of *Annie Get Your Gun*. N. P. 17 May 1946. Unidentified clipping in the Museum of the City of New York, Theatre Collection.

B325   ---------------. *Matinee Tomorrow: Fifty Years of Our Theatre*. New York: Whittlesey House, 1949.

B326   Morrison, Hobe. "Gershwin Memorial Cracks Stadium Records But Performances In and Out." *Variety* 11 Aug. 1937: A48, 1.

"Of all the evening's disappointments, Ethel Merman was the most notable. For one thing, only one of her selections was well suited to her brand of singing. For another, the Philharmonic Orchestra was woefully inadequate for the uplifting rhythms which only Miss Merman is able to arouse in a song. And for a third, the singer was inclined to be nervous in such strange surroundings and before such an awesome audience."

B327   Morrow, Lee Alan. *The Tony Award Book: Four Decades of Great American Theater*. New York: Abbeville Press, 1987. pp. 46-47, 49, 126, 127, 131, 142, 217

In addition to a brief biography of Merman, the book contains photographs of her in *Stage Door Canteen*, *Call Me Madam*, and *Gypsy*. She is also shown in rehearsal with Irving Berlin.

B328   "Movie Review." Rev. of *Call Me Madam*. *Look* 17 (5 May 1953): 100, 102, 103.

"Like other miracles, Ethel Merman has to be seen and heard to be believed."

B329   Nathan, George Jean. "Du Barry Was a Lonsdale." Rev. of *Du Barry Was a Lady*. *Newsweek* 14 (18 Dec. 1939): 35.

B330   Nelson, Stephen. *"Only a Paper Moon": The Theatre of Billy Rose*. Ann Arbor, MI: UMI Research Press, 1987. p. 93

Nelson mentions Merman's wartime appearance at the Diamond Horseshoe in the *It's Fun to Be Free* show; she sang "Any Bonds Today?"

B331   Nesbitt, Cathleen. *A Little Love and Good Company*. London: Faber and Faber, 1975. p. 235

"But oh! how my heart goes out to those oldtimers, from Sybil Thorndike to Ethel Merman who can advance on a stage without that trailing snake of a microphone, and speak to you and me instead of into its toadlike head."

B332   "New Acts: Palace, New York." *Variety* 17 Sept. 1930: A46, 5.

With remarkable prescience the reviewer noted about Merman, "When her singing some day is as genius-like as Siegel's playing and arranging, she will be set by herself."

B333   "New Musical on Broadway." Rev. of *Gypsy*. *Time* 73 (1 June 1959): 84.

Although the reviewer did not like the show, of Merman he wrote, "There is no more potent musicomedy fuel on Broadway than Ethel Merman, and she powers *Gypsy* with 50 million pounds of personality thrust."

B334   Nichols, Lewis. "Annie Get Your Gun." Rev. of *Annie Get Your Gun*. *New York Times* 17 May 1946: A14, 2.

"Miss Merman would be a professional in any surroundings whatsoever, but here they are made to order. . . . To say that Miss Merman has a way with a song is to understate the matter both quantitatively and qualitatively. . . . No one has ever failed to hear Ethel Merman, or to miss the glint in her eye. . . . Polished, winning, forthright and energetic, Miss Merman is the essence of the professional musical comedy player."

B335   --------------. "The Play: Something for the Boys." Rev. of *Something for the Boys*. *New York Times* 8 Jan. 1943: A24, 2, 3.

". . . Ethel Merman gives a performance that suggests that all Merman performances before last night were simply practice."

B336   Norden, Helen B. Review of *Kid Millions*. *Vanity Fair* 43 (Dec. 1934): 51.

B337   Norton, Elliot. *Broadway Down East: An Informal Account of the Plays, Players and Playhouses of Boston from Puritan Times to the Present*. Boston: Trustees of the Boston Public Library, 1978. pp. 73, 118

Norton credits Merman, among others, with creating an interest in the stage romances of middle-aged people.

B338   Notarius, Louis. "Short Reviews of Short Features. Rev. of *The Cave*

Club. *Publix Opinion* 27 June 1930:
A7, 4.

This reviewer concluded that the film
"should open the front show since it is not
strong enough to hold the closing spot on the
program." Of the actors, only Marjorie Leach
is mentioned by name.

B339   "Nothing Can Stop Her Now." *Sym-
           phony News* (December 1979): 42.

B340   Nugent, Frank S.   "The Screen."
           Rev. of *Strike Me Pink*. *New York
           Times* 17 Jan. 1936: A15, 2.

Nugent applauds "the always pleasant
singing of Ethel Merman."

B341   ---------------.   "The Screen."
           Rev. of *Anything Goes*. *New York
           Times* 6 Feb. 1936: A23, 3.

The film features "a Chinese extravaganza
and a nightclub sequence, both presenting Miss
Merman, happily."

B342   Nugent, John C. *It's a Great Life*.
           New York: Dial Press, 1940. p. 265

Nugent writes briefly of his appearance
in *Humpty Dumpty*.

B343   O'Connor, John J.   "Ed Sullivan's
           Broadway." *New York Times* 16 Mar.
           1973: A83, 2-4.

Here O'Connor writes, "At its second
best, the show unleashes Ethel Merman."

B344   ---------------.   "Survey of
           American Musical Comedy." *New York
           Times* 1 Oct. 1979: C17, 1-4.

O'Connor, who more than once was critical of Merman, writes, "And then there is Ethel Merman, the Everest of American musical comedy simply because she's there. I don't know how old Miss Merman is, and I don't care. She is a phenomenon, an event to be treasured. The simple facts are astonishing enough. . . . Standing on the stage as if she would slug the first numbskull who tried to move into her territory, Miss Merman belts simply away. The gestures are marvelously perfunctory, the presence has all the subtlety of a block of marble, but the voice is still thrilling and always unforgettable."

B345   ----------------.   "Television: Crosby and Knight Specials Fail Despite All Good Intentions." *New York Times* 30 Nov. 1976: A78, 3-4.

On Ted Knight's special, Merman, playing a schoolteacher, sang "There's No Business Like Show Business" and "God Bless America."

B346   ----------------.   "Television: Watching Thomas to Astaire to Hope to Bunker." *New York Times* 19 Jan. 1972: A38, 1-4.

In his response to *'S Wonderful*, O'Connor refers to "the jarring bellowing of Ethel Merman."

B347   "Obituary." *Maclean's* 97 (27 Feb. 1984): 4.

B348   "Obituary." *National Review* 36 (23 Mar. 1984): 16-17.

B349   "Obituary." *Newsweek* 103 (27 Feb. 1984): 76.

B350   "Obituary." *Time* 123 (27 Feb. 1984): 104.

B351   "On Broadway." Rev. of *Gypsy*. *Theatre Arts* 43 (Aug. 1959): 9, 72.

B352   "On the Current Screen." Rev. of
Strike Me Pink. *Literary Digest*
121 (25 June 1936): 19.

The only reference to Merman deplores the
cinematographic "artiness" of her musical
number.

B353   Oppenheimer, George. *The Passionate
Playgoer: A Personal Scrapbook*. New
York: Viking Press, 1958. pp. 70,
133, 213, 500-501

B354   Oppenheimer, Jerry and Jack Vitek.
Idol: Rock Hudson. New York: Vil-
lard Books, 1986. p. 179

The authors write of Hudson's televised
appearance with Merman on *Musical Comedy
Tonight*.

B355   "Owners of 46th St. Theatre Are Ne-
gotiating for Its Sale, But Theatre
Will Be Renamed for Ethel Merman in
October." *New York Times* 10 Sept.
1980: A24, 4.

Nothing came of this (or another similar)
idea.

B356   Parish, James R. and Vincent Ter-
race. *The Complete Actors' Television Credits, 1948-1988*. 2nd ed.
Vol. 2: Actresses. Metuchen, NJ:
Scarecrow Press, 1990. pp. 249-250

B357   ---------------- and Michael R.
Pitts. "Ethel Merman," *The Hol-
lywood Songsters* (New York: Garland
Publishing Co., 1990): 470-478.

B358   Parker, John, ed. *The Dramatic List: Who's Who in the Theatre: A Biographical Record of the Contemporary Stage*, 8th ed. London: Pitman, 1936. p. 1059

This is the first edition of this important reference book to list Merman's name. Parker errs in listing *Too Much Harmony* as one of Merman's films. He clearly misread the review of the film in the *New York Times* which noticed Merman's appearance in the accompanying stage show.

B359   Pastos, Spero. *Pin-Up: The Tragedy of Betty Grable*. New York: G. P. Putnam's Sons, 1986. pp. 40, 42

Grable, already established in films, appeared in *Du Barry Was a Lady*.

B360   Pavarotti, Luciano. *My Own Story*. Garden City, NY: Doubleday and Co., 1981. p. 131

Pavarotti discusses the phenomenal lack of *passagio* in Merman's voice as she goes from low to normal to high register.

B361   Payn, Graham and Sheridan Morley. *The Noël Coward Diaries*. Boston: Little, Brown and Co., 1982. pp. 80, 155, 192, 272, 407

B362   Payne, Robert. *Gershwin*. New York: Pyramid Books, 1960. pp. 114-116

B363   Pennington, Ron. "Ethel Merman." *Hollywood Reporter* 15 Aug. 1978.

B364   "People." *Time* 109 (30 May 1977): 71.

B365   "Peter Rogers, Who Created Ads Featuring Famous People Wearing Black-
glama Fur Coats, Publishes Book."
New York Times 18 Oct. 1980: A28,
6.

B366   Phillips, McCandlish.   "Broadway
Bids 'Dolly!' a Fond Adieu."   *New
York Times* 28 Dec. 1970: A38, 1-4.

B367   ---------------------. "'Sticks and
Stones.' 'Verona' Win Tonys." *New
York Times* 24 Apr. 1972: A40, 1.

"The house was roused to standing ova-
tions twice at the appearance of the special
award winners, Richard Rodgers and Ethel Merman, two of the fixed stars of the musical
theater."

B368   "Plays and Pictures."   Rev. of
Strike Me Pink. *New Statesman and
Nation* 11 (21 Mar. 1936): 457-458.

B369   "Plays on Broadway: Girl Crazy."
Rev. of *Girl Crazy. Variety* 22
Oct. 1930: A70, 3.

Herein Sime Silverman praises Merman's
performance and observes that she "may stand
up, but she needs to lose her automaton style
and give the ballads or rags more expression."

B370   "Plays on Broadway: Scandals." Rev.
of *George White's Scandals. Variety*
22 Sept. 1931: A54, 1.

"The times themselves are as much re-
sponsible for their [Merman's songs'] Apollo
popularity as Miss Merman, leaving the con-
jecture that this girl needs an emphatic bit
of ensemble behind her to punch across."

B371   "Plays on Broadway." Rev. of *Take a Chance*. *Variety* 29 Nov. 1932: A46, 4-5.

The reviewer speaks of Merman's "cobalt voice."

B372   "Plays out of Town: Humpty Dumpty." Rev. of *Humpty Dumpty*. *Variety* 20 Sept. 1932: A43, 1.

B373   "Plays out of Town: Take a Chance. Rev. of *Take a Chance*. *Variety* 15 Nov. 1932: A48, 5.

B374   Pleasants, Henry. *Great American Popular Singers*. New York: Simon and Schuster, 1974. pp. 333-342

B375   Poling, James. "Smile When You Call Merman Madam." *Collier's* 126 (12 Oct. 1950): 22-23.

B376   Pollock, Arthur. "Stars in Your Eyes." Rev. of *Stars in Your Eyes*. (Brooklyn, NY) *Eagle* Feb. 1939.

B377   Porter, A.   "Sure Shot Merman." *Collier's* 118 (10 Aug. 1946): 20, 21, 82-84.

B378   Porter, Cole. "Notes on the Morning after an Opening Night." *New York Times* 8 Nov. 1936.
". . . I'd rather write for Ethel than anyone else in the world. Every composer has his favorite, and she is mine. Her voice, to me, is thrilling. She has the finest enunciation of any American singer I know. She has a sense of rhythm which few can equal."

B379   "Portrait." *Harper's Bazaar* 80 (June 1946): 110.

This is Louise Dahl-Wolfe's photograph of Merman in *Annie Get Your Gun.*

B380   "Portrait."   *Holiday*   1   (Oct. 1946): 47.

Merman is depicted in *Annie Get Your Gun.*

B381   "Portrait."   *Life*   7   (11   Dec. 1939): 88-89.

Merman is depicted in *Du Barry Was a Lady.*

B382   "Portrait."   *Life*   9   (28   Oct. 1940): 67-68.

Merman is depicted in *Panama Hattie.*

B383   "Portrait."   *Life*   9   (30   Dec. 1940): 52.

Merman is depicted in *Panama Hattie.*

B384   "Portrait."   *Life*   14   (8   Feb. 1943): 79, 81.

Merman is depicted in *Something for the Boys.*

B385   "Portrait."   *Life* 20 (3 June 1946): 89, 91, 93.

Merman is depicted in *Annie Get Your Gun.*

B386   "Portrait."   *New York Times*   5 May 1935:   J9, 3-4.

The caption announces that Merman will sing on Sunday evenings on WABC-Radio with Al Goodman's Orchestra.

B387   "Portrait."   *New York Times*   17 Mar. 1960: A16, 4-5.

Merman is shown with Richard M. Nixon at a party given by the New York chapter of Variety Clubs International.

B388   "Portrait." *New York Times*   13 Oct. 1980: C11, 1.

Merman attended Helen Hayes' eightieth birthday party at the Actors' Fund Home.

B389   "Portrait." *Motion Picture*   51 (Feb. 1936): 29.

Merman and others in *Anything Goes* are shown.

B390   "Portrait." *Photoplay*   47 (Dec. 1934): 23.

Merman is shown with Eddie Cantor in *Kid Millions*.

B391   "Portrait." *Photoplay*   48 (Nov. 1935): 58.

B392   "Portrait." *Photoplay*   54 (May 1940): 52.

Merman is shown in *Du Barry Was a Lady*.

B393   "Portrait." *Publisher's Weekly* 154 (4 Dec. 1948): 2277.

Merman is shown with author James Michener.

B394   "Portrait." *Senior Scholastic* (27 Sept. 1957): 23+.

B395   "Portrait." *Stage* 13 (Jan. 1936): 63.

This is a handsome still photograph by Maurice Goldberg of Merman in the film *Anything Goes*.

B396   "Portrait." *Stage* 13 (Apr. 1936): 9.

Although this is really an advertisement for Chaubert's Drumbeat Perfume, the sultry photograph of Merman (from *Strike Me Pink*) is extremely striking.

B397   "Portrait." *Stage* 13 (Sept. 1936): front cover.

Gray-O'Reilly capture Merman in a colored action photograph from *Red, Hot, and Blue!*.

B398   "Portrait." *Stage* 14 (Nov. 1936): 90.

This candid photograph by André da Miano catches Merman in a handsome wedding dress and bouquet made of ermine for *Red, Hot, and Blue!* This issue also contains Merman's pictorial endorsement of Lux Soap (p. 79) and her selection as number one theatrical attraction by the Waldorf-Astoria Hotel (p. 23).

B399   "Portrait." *Stage* 15 (Aug. 1938): 44, 59.

B400   "Portrait." *Stage* 16 (Dec. 1938): cover.

B401   "Portrait." *Stage* 16 (15 Apr. 1939): 42.

B402   "Portrait." *Stage* 17 (1 Nov. 1940): 1.

B403   "Portrait." *Stage* 17 (1 Dec. 1940): cover, 35.

B404   "Portrait." *Theatre*   53 (Apr. 1931): 28.

B405   "Portrait." *Theatre Arts* 24 (Dec. 1940): frontispiece.

Merman and Rags Ragland are shown in *Panama Hattie*.

B406   "Portrait." *Theatre Arts* 24 (Jan. 1940): 49.

Merman and Bert Lahr are shown in *Du Barry Was a Lady*.

B407   "Portrait." *Theatre Arts* 25 (Jan. 1941): 8.

Merman and Joan Carroll are shown in *Panama Hattie*.

B408   "Portrait." *Theatre Arts* 30 (Aug. 1946): 474.

Merman is shown in *Annie Get Your Gun*.

B409   "Portrait." *Theatre Arts* 34 (Nov. 1950): 16.

Merman is shown in *Call Me Madam*.

B410   "Portrait." *The Times* (London) 30 Nov. 1972: AI, 3-5.

Merman is depicted singing "Katie Went to Haiti" in *Du Barry Was a Lady* in 1939.

B411   "Portrait." *Vanity Fair* 35 (Feb. 1931): 67.

A scene from *Girl Crazy* is depicted.

B412   "Portrait." *Vogue*   77 (15 Mar. 1931): 86.

B413   "Portrait." *Vogue* 101 (1 Mar. 1943): 52-53.

Merman is shown in *Something for the Boys.*

B414   "Portrait." *Vogue* 128 (Dec. 1956): 111.

Merman is shown in *Happy Hunting.*

B415   Preminger, Erik Lee. *Gypsy and Me: At Home and on the Road with Gypsy Rose Lee.* New York: Ballantine Books, 1984. pp. 113, 126

Preminger cites Lee's belief that her mother would have enjoyed seeing herself played by Merman.

B416   "The Pride of Astoria." *New York Times* 28 Dec. 1930: H3, 1-3.

B417   Prideaux, Tom. "At 78, Berlin Gives 'Annie' a New Showstopper-- and Is Pleased with Himself." Rev. of *Annie Get Your Gun.* *Life* 60 (10 June 1966): 47.

B418   "Production Dims Stars on 'Chevy Show." *New York Times* (7 Dec. 1955): A79, 2.

The show was overproduced and amateurish. ". . . Miss Merman is a lady who can stand up and slay audiences without any covering fire from a bandstand. Occasionally she was able to rise above the orchestral interference last night and then sounded fine."

B419   R., G. "Take a Chance Drips with Humor and Melody." Rev. of *Take a Chance.* (NY) *World-Telegram* 28 Nov. 1932.

B420   "Radio and Television: Female of the Species." *Time* 54 (15 Aug. 1949): 48, 2-3; 50, 3.

In this review of *The Ethel Merman Show*, Merman is favorably compared with the great radio comedians.

B421   "Radio Follow-Up: *The Big Show*." *Variety* (7 Mar. 1951): A34, 3.

Merman's songs are "particularly appealing."

B422   "Radio Follow-Up." *Variety* (17 Oct. 1951): A26, 3.

The Big Show (14 Oct. 1951) is noticed.

B423   "Radio Follow-Up: *The Big Show*." *Variety* (6 Feb. 1952): A34, 3.

The program was "enlivened by the verbal jousts" of Merman and Tallulah Bankhead. As to Merman's singing, "There is a wealth of showmanship in her offerings."

B424   "Radio Follow-Up: *The Big Show*." *Variety* (23 Apr. 1952): A30, 3.

B425   "Radio Reports: Gus Van." *Variety* 7 Jan. 1931: A72, 2.

Merman's guest appearance on Gus Van's show is noted.

B426   "Radio Reports: Rhythm at 8." *Variety* 15 May 1935: A42, 1.

In this format, Merman selects one of her hit songs, tells a story about it, and finally sings it. "Eadie Was a Lady" and "Hosannah" make the first program "a nifty 30 minutes." Ted Husing serves as emcee. "Miss Merman has also developed into a comedienne herself with a Mae Westian tinge which relays well."

B427   "Radio Reports: Ad Plugs." *Variety* 29 May 1935: A45, 3.

Noting that *Rhythm at 8* is sponsored by Lysol, the writer cautions against referring to Merman as "The Lysol Girl," which could lead to jokes that might destroy her career in radio.

B428   "Radio Reviews: *Keep 'Em Rolling*." *Variety* (12 Nov. 1941): A39, 2.

". . . Miss Merman's rhythm style infused the number ["The Flame of Freedom Is Burning"] with genuine lift."

B429   "Radio Reviews: *The Big Show*." *Variety* (8 Nov. 1950): A38, 1.

Merman's participation in the inaugural program is described.

B430   "Radio Reviews: *The Big Show*." *Variety* (2 May 1951): 30, 2.

B431   "Radio Reviews: *Jack Benny Salute*." *Variety* (14 Nov. 1951): A34, 1.

Merman's "socko moments" helped to make the program "one of the comedy delights of the radio season."

B432   Rathbun, Stephen. "Girl Crazy Scores." Rev. of *Girl Crazy*. (NY) *Sun* 15 Oct. 1930.

The reviewer thought it "difficult to discover any flaws in this musical comedy gem. . . ."

B433   *"Red, Hot, and Blue!" Stage* (Nov. 1936): 44-45.

This article features performance photographs by Jerome Robinson.

B434   Rev. of *Stage Door Canteen. Cosmopolitan* 114 (June 1943): 66.

B435   Rev. of *Stage Door Canteen. Photoplay* 23 (Aug. 1943): 22.

B436   Rev. of *Annie Get Your Gun. Modern Music* 23, 2 (Apr. 1946): 144.

B437   Rev. of *Call Me Madam. Christian Science Monthly Magazine* 21 Oct. 1950: 6.

B438   Rev. of *Call Me Madam. Collier's* 126 (21 Oct. 1950): 22-23.

B439   Rev. of *Call Me Madam. Theatre Arts* 34 (Dec. 1950): 15.

Merman is compared with "a strangely subtle bulldozer."

B440   Rev. of *Gypsy. Vogue* 134 (July 1959): 60-61.

B441   Rev. of *Happy Hunting. The Reporter* 16 (24 Jan. 1957): 35.

Merman was "everything that her special raucous ebullient genius should be."

B442   Rev. of *Something for the Boys. Time* 41 (18 Jan. 1943): 58.

B443   Rev. of *The Tony Awards. Variety* 26 Apr. 1972: A38, 1.

"The Merman medley found the longtime musical favorite rising to the occasion, as she always has, and belting out her past winners with typical verve, her voice sounding best in 'Annie Get Your Gun' and 'Call Me Madam' excerpts. Hal Linden and Larry Blyden were expert assistants in making the Merman segment work theatrically and emotionally."

B444   Rev. of *There's No Business Like Show Business*. *Dance Magazine* 29 (9 Jan. 1955): 9.

B445   Reynolds, Debbie and David P. Columbia. *Debbie*. New York: Pocket Books, 1980. pp. 161, 416

B446   "'Rhythm' from Coast If Pic Jobs for Tops." *Variety* 29 May 1935: A39, 5.

Merman's radio show *Rhythm at 8* may be broadcasted from Los Angeles after 15 July if her associates Ted Husing and bandleader Al Goodman find film work and follow Merman to Hollywood. [As it happened, Goodman remained in New York and conducted the program on his own.]

B447   Robbins, Jhan. *Inka Dinka Doo: The Life of Jimmy Durante*. New York: Paragon House, 1991. pp. 117, 119, 121, 176

B448   Robe, Lucy B. *Co-Starring Famous Women and Alcohol*. Minneapolis, MN: CompCare Publications, 1986. pp. 54-55, 168, 173, 201, 242, 267

"An Ethel Merman show would, indeed, go on--but at what price to its alcoholic star, who must have believed that because she controlled *when* she drank she could not have a problem with alcohol?"

B449   Roeder, Bill. "Newsmakers." *Newsweek* 89 (7 Mar. 1977): 52.

This note, advertising the forthcoming
Together on Broadway, gives anecdotes about
Merman's friendship with Mary Martin.

B450   ------------. "Newsmakers."
Newsweek 89 (30 May 1977): 52.

The writer offers a glowing response to
Together on Broadway.

B451   Rogers, Ginger. *Ginger: My Story.*
New York: HarperCollins, 1991. pp.
69, 74

Rogers writes that her mother Lela McMath
Rogers suggested that Vinton Freedley audition
Merman for *Girl Crazy*.

B452   Rogow, L. "Brassy Dame." *Saturday
Review* 38 (2 July 1955): 27.

B453   Rose. Rev. of *The Gershwin Years*.
Variety 18 Jan. 1961: A38, 1.

The reviewer's conclusion is that the
show was good but technically over-produced.

B454   Rosen, George. "Ford's Half-Century
TV Cavalcade a 500G, 2-Web, Star-
Studded Jubilee." *Variety* (17
June 1953): A27, 4.

"It's not surprising that the Ethel Mer-
man-Mary Martin contribs highlighted the evening's entertainment. . . ."

B455   Ross, --. "Stars in Your Eyes."
Rev. of *Stars in Your Eyes*. (NY)
World-Telegram Feb. 1939.

B456   Rothstein, Edward. "Ethel Merman: I Guess I'm Blessed with Good Lungs." *New York Times* 9 May 1982: B1, 1-3; B22, 1-6.

B457   "Royal Variety Performance Adds $425,000 to U. K. Artists' Fund." *Variety* 17 Nov. 1982: A2, 4.

"Female performing ability was much in evidence. Ethel Merman came from U. S. to give a rousing finale performance of "There's No Business Like Show Business."

B458   Ruhl, Arthur. Rev. of *Girl Crazy*. (NY) *Tribune* 15 Oct. 1930.

Merman's performance is characterized by "dash, authority, good voice and just the right knowing style."

B459   Russell, Rosalind and Chris Chase. *Life Is a Banquet*. NY: Random House, 1977. pp. 197, 202

Russell thinks her friend Merman should have recreated her stage role in the film of *Gypsy*.

B460   Sanders, Coyne S. *Rainbow's End: The Judy Garland Show*. New York: William Morrow, 1990. pp. 40, 123, 126, 207, 212-214, 262, 295, 297, 299, 300-301, 341

Sanders gives a complete account of Merman's appearances on Judy Garland's wonderful but ill-fated TV show.

B461   Schonberg, Harold C.   "Inaugural Spotlight Shifts to Sinatra and Show Biz." *New York Times* 20 Jan. 1981: B2, 1.

Merman was among the entertainers who performed on 18 January as part of Reagan's inaugural celebrations.

B462   Schumach, Murray. "Ethel Merman, Queen of Musical Stage, Dies at 76," *New York Times* 16 February 1984: A1, D26.

B463   Schwartz, Charles. *Cole Porter.* New York: Dial Press, 1977.

B464   Seaman, Barbara. *Lovely Me: The Life of Jacqueline Susann.* New York: William Morrow, 1987. pp. 144, 244, 247, 248, 289, 290, 311-312, 440

Seaman suggests that Susann's unflattering portrait of Helen Lawson, a Merman-like character in *Valley of the Dolls*, resulted in the singer's rejection of the homosexual attentions of the writer.

B465   Segal, Lewis. "Merman Sings at Hollywood Bowl." *Los Angeles Times* 8 Aug. 1977: D12, 3.

B466   Seligsohn, Leo. "Ethel Merman." *Long Island Newsday* 1 Mar. 1981: A2, 22, 24, 25, 29.

B467   Settel, Irving and William Laas. *A Pictorial History of Television.* New York: Grosset and Dunlap, 1969. p. 86

One of the authors was in the studio audience during the telecast of the Ford 50th Anniversary Special.

B468   Shanley, J. P. "Miss Merman and Miss M'Kenna in New Roles." *New*

York Times   25 Mar. 1956:   B13, 1-2.

The author writes of Merman's straight dramatic roles in two TV plays.

B469   --------------.   "TV: Shower of Stars." *New York Times*   10 June 1955: A45, 2, 3.

The stars in this case included Edgar Bergen, Dan Dailey, Betty Grable, Red Skelton, Harry James, Shirley MacLaine, Marilyn Maxwell, Jack Oakie, Gene Nelson, and child dancer Patricia Rosemond. In her first spot, Merman sang "Over the Rainbow" but was considered to have excelled later with "You're the Top."

B470   Shaw, Arnold. *The Jazz Age: Popular Music in the 1920's*.   New York: Oxford UP, 1987.   pp. 238, 275, 283

Shaw writes of "a brass section known as Ethel Merman."

B471   Sheed, Wilfrid. "The Stage." Rev. of *Annie Get Your Gun*. *Commonweal* 84 (24 June 1966): 393-394.

Merman is "a little older but still in her elastic prime."

B472   "Show Business: Nightclubs: Delicious, Delectable, De-Lovely." *Time* 22 Nov. 1963: 78.

In this review of Merman's concert engagement at the Persian Room of New York's Plaza Hotel, Merman "says she is through with Broadway, which ties her down too much, and her fans will have to take her in solo, con-

centrated form from now on, in these retro-
spective nightclub shows."

B473   "Show on Broadway." Rev. of *Happy
             Hunting. Variety*   12 Dec. 1956:
             A72, 1-2.

Merman has "a voice like a calliope, the
energy of a bulldozer and the comedy touch of
an old pro."

B474   "Show on Broadway." Rev. of *Annie
             Get Your Gun. Variety* 8 June 1966:
             A54, 4-5.

Merman's "amazing voice seems to have all
its old natural quality, and she puts over
every song, gets every laugh and holds the
audience every moment."

B475   "Show out of Town." Rev. of *Gypsy.
             Variety*, 15 Apr. 1959: A150, 4-5.

"In addition to demonstrating once again
her infallible ability to bang across a song
number, . . . Miss Merman takes time off to
create and establish a real character. . . ."

B476   "Show out of Town: Happy Hunting.
             Rev. of *Happy Hunting. Variety* 24
             Oct. 1956: A70, 1-2.

B477   Sillman, Leonard. *Here Lies Leonard
             Sillman: Straightened out at Last.*
             New York: Citadel Press, 1959. pp.
             268-269

Sillman describes a rehearsal for a benefit in 1937 in which Merman's iron-willed pro-
fessionalism was interpreted as gaucherie.

B478   Simon, George T. *Best of the Music
             Makers.* Garden City, NY: Doubleday
             and Co., 1979. pp. 394-396

B479   "Singers Frank Sinatra and Ethel Merman and Part-Time Song-Writer Otis Blackwell to Be Presented with National Academy of Pop Music's 1st Johnny Mercer Awards on Mar. 17." *New York Times* (13 Mar. 1980): C21, 3.

B480   "Sketch." *Photoplay* 46 (July 1934): 79.

B481   Skinner, Cornelia Otis. *Life with Lindsay and Crouse*. Boston: Houghton Mifflin, 1976. pp. 154, 156-157, 158, 159-160, 161-163, 210-211, 213, 219

B482   Smith, Cecil M. *Musical Comedy in America*. New York: Theatre Arts Books, 1950. pp. 86, 267, 270, 301, 310-312, 318, 323-324

B483   Sobel, Bernard. *A Pictorial History of Burlesque*. New York: Bonanza Books, 1956. p. 161

Sobel argues that Merman's duet with child actress Joan Carroll in *Panama Hattie* (Sobel incorrectly identifies the show as *Call Me Madam*) was presaged by Anna Held in a similar situation in a much earlier show.

B484   Spaeth, Sigmund. *A History of Popular Music in America*. pp. 462, 480, 490, 499, 500

B485   Spitzer, Marian. *The Palace*. New York: Atheneum, 1969. pp. 168, 170, 181, 191, 194, 252

Merman played the Palace with Clayton, Jackson, and Durante and again (11 July to 18 September 1931) after her triumph in *Girl Crazy*. Afterwards she performed there several

times. Merman was in the audience at the closing of the theatre on 29 January 1966.

B486   "Stage: Tragedy Makes 'Anything
             Goes' Funniest Hit of the Year."
             Rev. of *Anything Goes*. *Newsweek* 4
             (1 Dec. 1934): 23.

B487   "Star's Operation." *The Times*
             (London) 18 Apr. 1983: A1, 1.

B488   Stickney, Dorothy. *Openings and
             Closings*. Garden City, NY: Dou-
             bleday and Co., 1979. pp. 95, 104,
             151, 153

B489   Stott, Jane and William Stott. *On
             Broadway*. Austin: University of
             Texas Press, 1978. pp. xxvii,
             xxviii, xxix, xxxiii, 4, 54, 74,
             93, 128, 170, 171, 232, 291, 292,
             328, 337

B490   "Strippers Have Culture Too: 'Gyp-
             sy' Gals Hold Art Exhibit." *Thea-
             tre* Nov. 1959.

The show's strippers whiled away their
backstage hours by painting, the fruits of
which were sold at a charity auction. Merman
was among the first to make a purchase.

B491   "Students Honor Ethel Merman." *New
             York Times* 12 Mar. 1966: A13, 1.

Harvard's Hasty Pudding Club named Merman
Woman of the Year.

B492   "Surgery for Merman." *New York
             Times* 13 Aug. 1955: A7, 2.

The nature of the complaint that prompted
out-patient surgery in Denver, CO, is not revealed; nor does Merman give any clue in her
autobiography.

B493   Sutton, Larry. "Ethel Merman Dies at 75." (NY) *Daily News*   16 Feb. 1984.

B494   Swain, Joseph P. *The Broadway Musical: A Critical and Musical Survey*. New York: Oxford University Press, 1990.   pp. 130, 152, 293, 319, 320, 321, 331, 372

Although this book examines music rather than performers, it is useful in terms of evaluating the musical demands of some of Merman's scores.

B495   Swanberg, W. A.   *Luce and His Empire*.   New York: Dell Publishing Co., 1973. p. 170

B496   Swindell, Larry.   *Screwball: The Life of Carole Lombard*.   New York: William Morrow, 1975.   pp. 99, 137

B497   "The Talk of the Town: What Comes Naturally." Rev. of *Annie Get Your Gun*. *New Yorker*   22 (22 June 1946): 20-21.

Merman's voice is "an instrument of untrammelled resonance."

B498   "Talking Shorts: Ethel Merman, Ireno." Rev. of *Ireno*. *Variety*   7 June 1932: A20, 1.

The reviewer concludes that the film is "fine."

B499   "Talking Shorts: Ethel Merman, Let Me Call You Sweetheart." Rev. of *Let Me Call You Sweetheart*. *Variety*   26 July 1932: A17, 1.

The reviewer praises this blending of a "name" singer and a Betty Boop cartoon. "Recommended as a valuable program adjunct anywhere."

B500   "Talking Shorts: Ethel Merman, Song Shopping." Rev. of *Song Shopping*. *Variety* 9 May 1933: A14, 3.

"Miss Merman's song salesmanship is the best part of the short."

B501   "Talking Shorts: Ethel Merman, Time on My Hands." Rev. of *Time on My Hands*. *Variety* 3 Jan. 1933: A19, 2.

The film is "nicely handled with pretty good results."

B502   Taylor, Robert. *Fred Allen: His Life and Wit*. Boston: Little, Brown and Co., 1989. p. 292

B503   Taylor, Theodore. *Jule: The Story of Composer Jule Styne*. New York: Random House, 1979. pp. 10, 63, 174, 177-178, 182, 196-198, 200-205, 208-212, 216-218, 220, 262, 269-271, 273, 274

B504   "Tele Follow-Up Comment: *Milton Berle*." *Variety* (30 Mar. 1949): A30, 4.

Merman and Berle's song-and-dance routine of "Friendship" was "the hour's top item."

B505   "Tele Follow-Up Comment: *Ford Show*." *Variety* (22 June 1949): A30, 5.

Merman and Lauritz Melchior's "dueting did nothing to enhance their TV prestige."

B506   "Tele Follow-Up Comment: *The Chevy Show*." *Variety* (14 Dec. 1955): A35, 3.

The show had problems that "even [Merman's] glossy showmanship couldn't overcome." Even so, "she is still the prize belter of the vigor set and caught the show's lustiest plaudits."

B507   "Tele Follow-Up Comment: *Perry Como Show*." *Variety* (11 Dec. 1957): A44, 4.

"Miss Merman whipped up a musical storm. . . . She supplied lotsa spark throughout."

B508   "Tele Follow-Up Comment." *Variety* (9 Oct. 1963): A36, 1.

Merman's appearance on *The Judy Garland Show* (6 Oct. 1963) is noticed.

B509   "Tele Follow-Up Comment: *Bell Telephone Hour*." *Variety* (5 Feb. 1964): A31, 4.

"The show got off the ground with the very first note Miss Merman trumpeted, so instant is her showmanship and so effectively does she project."

B510   "Tele Follow-Ups: *Ed Sullivan*." *Variety* (20 July 1955): A31, 3.

With the exception of Merman, it was a lackluster show.

B511   "Television Reviews: *That Girl*." *Variety* (13 Sept. 1967): A46, 3.

Merman "made the show hers with very little effort."

B512   "Television Reviews: *Musical Comedy
             Tonight.*" *Variety* (3 Oct. 1979):
             A58, 1.

Merman's name is conspicuous by its absence.

B513   "Theater: Navy Comes Back to Broad-
             way." Rev. of *Panama Hattie*, by
             Herbert Fields, B. G. De Sylva, and
             Cole Porter. *Life* 9 (28 Oct.
             1940): 67-68.

B514   "Theater: Something for the Boys."
             Rev. of *Something for the Boys*.
             Life 14 (8 Feb. 1943): 79, 81, 82.

B515   "Theater." Rev. of *Annie Get Your
             Gun*. *Life* 30 (3 June 1946): 89-
             94.

B516   "Theater: Annie Scores a Bull's-
             Eye." Rev. of *Annie Get Your Gun*.
             Newsweek 27 (27 May 1946): 84-85.

B517   "Theater: New Plays." Rev. of *Call
             Me Madam*. *Newsweek* 36 (23 Oct.
             1950): 84.

B518   "The Theater: New Musical in Man-
             hattan." Rev. of *Du Barry Was a
             Lady*. *Time* 34 (18 Dec. 1939): 45.

"Bert Lahr is at his best--which is good
enough. Ethel Merman is at her best--which is
tops." Her voice is likened to a "train announcer's contralto."

B519   "The Theater: New Musical in Man-
             hattan." Rev. of *Something for the*

Boys. *Time* 41 (18 Jan. 1943): 58,
1-3.

This review includes a photograph of Merman and Cole Porter.

B520   "The Theater: New Musical in Manhattan." Rev. of *Annie Get Your Gun*. *Time* 47 (27 May 1946): 66.

"Star, whip, and wheelhorse of *Annie* is Ethel Merman."

B521   "The Theater: New Musical in Manhattan." Rev. of *Call Me Madam*. *Time* 56 (23 Oct. 1950): 58.

". . . even when her [Merman's] material lays an egg, she makes it seem like a golden one."

B522   "The Theater: New Musical in Manhattan." Rev. of *Happy Hunting*. *Time* 68 (17 Dec. 1956): 62-63.

Merman "has the urgency of a steam calliope, the assurance of an empress, and a likable low-downness all her own."

B523   "The Theater: New Musical in Manhattan." Rev. of *Gypsy*. *Time* 73 (1 June 1959): 84-85.

". . . the trumpet-tonsilled Merman voice is always in the winner's circle."

B524   "The Theater: Porter on Panama." *Time* 36 (28 Oct. 1940): cover; 65, 1-3; 66, 3; 67, 1.

The cover depicts Merman as Panama Hattie.

B525   "They Rise and Shine." *Harper's Bazaar* 73 (Nov. 1939): 88-89.

Merman and Bert Lahr are depicted in *Du Barry Was a Lady*.

B526   Thomas, Bob. "Honeymoon Disaster Wrecked Ethel Merman's Marriage on Their Very First Night." *Star* 29 Oct. 1985: 33-36.

This article, distilled from Thomas' biography of Merman (**B527**), is one of a series published by the newspaper.

B527   -----------. *I Got Rhythm: The Ethel Merman Story*. New York: G. P. Putnam's Sons, 1985.

B528   -----------. "The Night Broadway Turned out Its Lights for Ethel Merman." *Star* 22 Oct. 1985: 22-23.

B529   "Thrift Shop Opening Is a Wild Scramble." *New York Times* 13 Nov. 1936: A25, 1.
Merman was to have opened the thrift shop that aided the Irvington House, but she was late.

B530   "The Times Diary: Ethel Merman's London Role." *The Times* (London) 29 July 1969: A6, 5-6.

Merman's negotiations to stage *Gypsy* in London are discussed. A photograph also appears.

B531   Todd, Michael, Jr. and Susan M. Todd. *A Valuable Property: The Life Story of Michael Todd*. New York: Arbor House, 1983. pp. 83-88

Writing of his father's contributions to
Something for the Boys, Todd cites interesting
examples of Merman's comedic ploys on stage.

B532   Tormé, Mel. *The Other Side of the
          Rainbow with Judy Garland on the
          Dawn Patrol*. New York: William
          Morrow, 1970. pp. 119-120

B533   Trau. Rev. of *Shower of Stars: The
          Showstoppers*. *Variety* 26 Jan.
          1955: A31, 5.

B534   Trau. Rev. of *Shower of Stars:
          Ethel Merman's Show Stoppers*. *Va-
          riety* 20 Apr. 1955, A30, 3.

B535   Trewin, Ion. "Ethel Merman: London
          Palladium." *The Times* (London) 10
          Sept. 1974: A10, 4-5.

Trewin offers a glowing review of Merman's concert in London's principal variety
venue.

B536   "TV: 'Big Event' Presented Live."
          New York Times 28 Sept. 1976: A77,
          1.

"Except for portions of the Broadway sec-
tion--most notably Ethel Merman singing in
Sardi's and Hal Linden performing in Shubert
Alley--the 90 minutes sank in a swamp of bored
bystanders and irritated personalities. . . ."

B537   "TV Followup Comment: Ed Sullivan,"
          Variety 14 Oct. 1959: A31, 1.

Complaining about the useless scenery
used in Merman's "I'm Glad There Is You," the
reviewer observes, "Ethel Merman was the big
gun. . . but she was not loaded properly."
Later he says, "Merman sings 'em straight and

hard and doesn't need any scene designer's frills to help her along."

B538   "TV Says It with Irving Berlin Music," *Variety* 8 May 1968: A228, 4.

"Miss Merman belted out 'There's No Business Like Show Business' and other songs with no audible or visible diminution of her customary vigor."

B539   Tynan, Kenneth. "Cornucopia." *New Yorker* 35 (30 May 1959): 65-67.

This review is included in the following item.

B540   --------------. *Curtains: Selections from the Drama Criticism and Related Writings*. New York: Atheneum, 1961. pp. 321, 322

In his review of *Gypsy*, Tynan wrote of ". . .Ethel Merman, the most relaxed brass section on earth, singing her heart out and missing none of her inimitable tricks, among them her habit of sliding down to important words from a grace note above, which supplies the flick that precedes the vocal whipcrack."

B541   "Union Apologizes to Ethel Merman." *New York Times* 27 Nov. 1957: A24, 5.

B542   Untermeyer, Louis. Jacket notes. *Annie Get Your Gun*. Decca Records DL 9018, 1946.

B543   ----------------. Jacket notes. *Call Me Madam*. Decca Records DL 5456, 1953.

B544   ----------------.   Jacket notes.
Ethel Merman: Memories.   Decca
Records DL 9028.

B545   ----------------.   Jacket notes.
*Ethel Merman: A Musical
Autobiography.* Decca Records DX
153, 1956.

B546   "Uris Hall of Fame Names First
Group." *New York Times* 27 Oct.
1972: A33, 1.

A panel of critics, editors, theatre his-
torians, and educators inducted 23 artists out
of 166 nominees into the Theater Hall of Fame
and Museum housed in the Uris Theater. Merman
is one of the honorees.

B547   Vallance, Tom. *The American Musical.* New York: A. S. Barnes, 1970.

B548   Vallée, Rudy. *Let the Chips Fall.
. .* Harrisburg, PA: Stackpole
Books, 1975. pp. 69, 71, 112

Vallée discusses Al Siegel's pride in the
accomplishment in *Girl Crazy* of his "discov-
ery," Merman. [At this stage in his life, Vallée used the acute accent in his name.]

B549   "Variety House Reviews: Paramount,
N. Y." *Variety* 26 Sept. 1933:
A13, 1.

In an eleven-minute program, Merman sang
a couple of songs and an encore. "They liked
her singing tremendously."

B550   "Variety House Reviews: Paramount,
N. Y." *Variety* 24 Apr. 1934: A49,
1.

Merman "opens with a medley of her hits, gets a hand in this and takes off her coat wrap to unveil a wonderful back. She got plenty more applauses [sic] for "Love Thy Neighbour," but she didn't take anything more off and she did not take an encore other than a couple of bows. Saving up." Later she sang "Eadie Was a Lady."

B551   "Variety House Reviews: Paramount, N. Y." *Variety* 15 Apr. 1936: A19, 2.

Merman sang "I Get a Kick out of You" and a medley of her hits.

B552   "Vaude House Reviews: Palace." *Variety* 26 Apr. 1932: A30, 3.

Attendance at this week's shows has not been good because the audience has "seen 'em too often." Of Merman's performance, however, the reviewer notes that her vocal delivery is "one of the few new things that have come along."

B553   Vernon, Grenville. "The Stage and Screen." Rev. of *Stars in Your Eyes. Commonweal* 29 (3 Mar. 1939): 525.

This reviewer is more concerned with morals than art.

B554   ----------------. "The Stage and Screen." Rev. of *Du Barry Was a Lady. Commonweal* 31 (29 Dec. 1939): 227.

According to Vernon, this show is "utterly lacking in decency."

B555 ------------------. "The Stage and Screen." Rev. of *Panama Hattie*. *Commonweal* 33 (15 Nov. 1940): 103.

Vernon writes of Merman's "saw-toothed voice."

B556 "Wagner Issues a Vacation Call as City Opens Summer Festival." *New York Times* 21 June 1957: A27, 6-7.

Merman was named official hostess of the festival and sang "Gee, But It's Good to Be Here" at the inaugural function.

B557 Waldorf, Wilella. "Girl Crazy Arrives." Rev. of *Girl Crazy*. *New York Post* 15 Oct. 1930.

B558 ----------------. "Two on the Aisle." Rev. of *Something for the Boys*. *New York Post* 8 Jan. 1943.

B559 ----------------. "Stars in Your Eyes Opens at the Majestic Theatre." Rev. of *Stars in Your Eyes*. *New York Post* 10 Feb. 1939.

"It may seem impossible, but we are of the opinion at the moment that Ethel Merman last night achieved the not inconsiderable feat of out-Mermaning Merman."

B560 Walsh, Moira. "Films." Rev. of *Call Me Madam*. *America* 89 (4 Apr. 1953): 25.

Merman is "altogether winning whether delivering a song or a badly rehearsed ambassadorial speech." The film is "inspired light entertainment."

B561 ------------. "Films." Rev. of *There's No Business Like Show*

Business. America 92 (18 Dec. 1954): 326.

The film is "entertaining and unusually credible."

B562   Waters, --. "Shows out of Town: Happy Hunting." Rev. of *Happy Hunting. Variety* 24 Oct. 1956.

B563   Watson, Thomas J. and Bill Chapman. *Judy: Portrait of an American Legend.* New York: McGraw-Hill, 1986. pp. 13, 58, 105, 111

B564   Watt, Douglas. "Her Brassy Voice Was Pure Gold." (NY) *Daily News* 16 Feb. 1984.

B565   Watts, Richard, Jr. "Ethel Merman Has Another Success." Rev. of *Gypsy. New York Post* 22 May 1959, in *New York Theatre Critics' Reviews* 1959: 300.

"The most challenging role Ethel Merman has ever faced is the ruthless stage mother in Gypsy, and she comes through triumphantly."

B566   ------------------. "New Hit." Rev. of *Du Barry Was a Lady.* (NY) *Herald-Tribune* 7 Dec. 1939.

Merman "plays the nightclub singer. . . with that engaging relish that makes her so irresistible an entertainer."

B567   ------------------. "The Theatres." Rev. of *Panama Hattie.* (NY) *Herald-Tribune* 31 Oct. 1940.

Merman is "even better than ever, which is saying something. It is hard to believe it, but I think that she sings more effectively, acts more engagingly and looks handsomer than in any of her previous shows."

B568   ------------------. "The Theatres."
             Rev. of *Red, Hot, and Blue!* (NY)
             Herald-Tribune 1 Nov. 1936.

     "Miss Merman sings as alluringly as ever.
. . ."

B569   ------------------. "The Theatres."
             Rev. of *Stars in Your Eyes.* (NY)
             Herald-Tribune 10 Feb. 1939.

B570   ------------------. "Two on the
             Aisle: Annie Once Again Gets Her
             Gun." Rev. of *Annie Get Your Gun.*
             Saturday Review 1 June 1966.

     "Time has neither withered nor staled Ethel Merman's infinite power as a singer and performer. . . . the dynamic Miss Merman, as usual, takes over the whole place and dominates the proceedings with her unrivaled authority. . . ."

B571   Whipple, Sidney. "Du Barry Was a
             Lady: New Musical Comedy." Rev. of
             Du Barry Was a Lady. (NY) *World-
             Telegram* 7 Dec. 1939.

B572   ---------------. "Panama Hattie Has
             All a Musical Needs." Rev. of *Pan-
             ama Hattie.* (NY) *World-Telegram* 31
             Oct. 1940.

     "The book doesn't really amount to much, but who cares so long as the Merman girl is on the stage with a song to sing and some expert clowning to do?"

B573   "White's Merman Deal Working in 3
             Ways." *Variety* 1 Sept. 1931: A52,
             4.

George White has either bought or borrowed Merman's contract from Freedley and Aarons.

B574   Whiting, Margaret and Will Holt. *It Might as Well Be Spring: A Musical Autobiography.* New York: William Morrow, 1987. pp. 12, 18-19, 28-29

Merman came to see Whiting's cabaret tribute to her four times. While working on *Take a Chance*, songwriter Richard Whiting quipped, "You should hear Merman's voice. It carries to the very last row in the balcony. And that's before she starts singing!"

B575   Wilk, Max. *Every Day's a Matinee: Memoirs Scribbled on a Dressing Room Door.* New York: W. W. Norton, 1975. pp. 88, 241, 253-254, 258, 259

On p. 241 there is a picture of Merman and Mary Martin rehearsing for the Ford 50th Anniversary television special.

B576   Wilson, John S. "Pop: Ethel Merman at Carnegie Hall," *New York Times* 12 May 1982: C25.

B577   Winchell, Walter. "New Big Hit at Apollo Funny Show." Rev. of *Take a Chance. The Mirror* 28 Nov. 1932.

The performance of "Eadie Was a Lady" and "You're an Old Smoothie" remind you that Ethel Merman is in herself an entertainment. . . ."

B578   Wodehouse, P. G. and Guy Bolton. *Bring on the Girls!: The Improbable Story of Our Life in Musical Comedy, with Pictures to Prove It.* New York: Simon and Schuster, 1953.

B579   Woolf, S. J. "Sharpshooting Singer from Astoria." *New York Times Magazine* 2 June 1946: 22, 1-4.

B580   "Writers of Musical." *Variety* 8 Apr. 1931: A60, 4.

Jack MacGowan and George and Ira Gershwin have been signed to write the new Merman musical.

B581   Wyatt, Euphemia V. "The Drama." Rev. of *Anything Goes*. *Catholic World* 140 (Jan. 1935): 469-470.

This reviewer demonstrably is more interested in exposing "vulgarity" than in evaluating art. Merman's name is not even mentioned.

B582   ------------------.   "The Drama." Rev. of *Red, Hot, and Blue!* *Catholic World* 144 (Dec. 1936): 338-339.

B583   ------------------.   "The Drama." Rev. of *Stars in Your Eyes*. *Catholic World* 149 (Apr. 1939): 525.

B584   ------------------.   "The Drama." Rev. of *Panama Hattie*. *Catholic World* 152 (Dec. 1940): 335.

B585   ------------------.   "The Drama." Rev. of *Something for the Boys*. *Catholic World* 156 (Feb. 1943): 601.

B586   ------------------.   "The Drama." Rev. of *Annie Get Your Gun*. *Catholic World* 163 (July 1946): 359.

B587   ------------------.   "Theater."
            Rev. of *Call Me Madam*. *Catholic
            World* 172 (Dec. 1950): 225.

B588   ------------------.   "Theater."
            Rev. of *Happy Hunting*. *Catholic
            World* 184 (Feb. 1957): 386.

B589   Young, Stark. "Seasonal Notes."
            New Republic 81 (12 Dec. 1934):
            131.

Young writes of Merman as "intelligent
and sharp."

B590   Zadan, Craig. *Sondheim and Company*.
            New York: Macmillan, 1974. pp. 37,
            38, 39, 40, 41, 43, 44, 46-50, 52,
            54, 55, 179, 202

B591   Zepernick, Werner.   "Ethel Merman
            Delights   Audience."   *Nashville
            Tennessean* 17 Sept. 1976.

B592   Zolotow, Maurice. *No People Like
            Show People*. New York: Random
            House, 1951. pp. 287-305

Index

Asner, Edward (1929--),
  T78
Astaire, Fred (1899-
  1987), T38
Aston, Frank (1897-
  1982), B17
Atkinson, Brooks (1894-
  1984), B18, B19, B20,
  B21, B22, B23, B24,
  B25, B26, B27, B28
Atlanta Symphony, S78,
  49
Aubert, Jeanne
  (1906--), S21
Austin, Irene, S28
Austin, John P., F26
Ayres, Mitchell
  (c. 1911-69), T38

Backus, Jim (1913-89),
  F24
Bacon, James (1914--),
  B29
Baird, Bobbi (d. 1937),
  S42
Bakaleinikoff, Constan-
  tin (c. 1898-1966),
  F21
Bakanic, Bob, S35
Baker, Benny (1907--),
  F15, S27
Baker, Beverly, S45
Baker, Jack, S28
Bal, Jeanne, S31
Baldwin, Franca, S30
Ball, Jane, S28
Ball, Lucille (1911-
  89), S27, T36, T107,
  17
Ballard, Kaye (1926--),
  T82
Ballard, Lucinda
  (1908--), S30
Baltimore Symphony,
  S79, 49
Banasse, O. J., S17
"Band Played On, The,"
  D32
Bankhead, Tallulah
  (1903-68), R16, R18,
  R19, R21, B30, B240
Banks, Diana, S42

Baral, Robert (1910--),
  B31
Barbara, Truly, S30
Barbee, Richard
  (1887--), S26
Barbier, George (1866-
  1945), F20
Barnes, Clive (1927--),
  B32
Barnes, Howard (1904-
  68), B33, B34, B35
Barnes Twins, S29
Barnett, Art, S30
Barrett, Jack
  (d. 1964), S10
Barrie, Leslie, S21
Barrie, Wendy (1912-
  78), F15
Barry, William
  (1911--), S21
Barter Theatre Award,
  B143, 18, 41
Barthel, Joan, B36
Bartis, Aristide, S31
Bass, Jules, T94
Bass, Saul (1920--),
  F24
Batman (TV), T46, T47,
  7, 44
Baxter, Beverley (1891-
  1964), B37
Bay, Howard (1912-86),
  S29
"Be a Witch," D43
Be Like Me (film), F10,
  34
Beaber, Jack, S30
Beard, James, S45
Beard, Stymie
  (d. 1981), F14
Beaumont, Gloria, S10
Becker, Edward, S35
"Before the Parade
  Passes By," T88
Begg, John (c. 1943-
  89), S30
Beggs, Lee (1870-1943),
  S18
Belasco, Leon (1902-
  88), F22, F26, S35,
  D36
Belfer, Hal (1927--),
  F26

Edens, Roger (c. 1906–70), S10, S11, S12, S13, S16, S32, T24

Edwards, Anne (1927--), B108, B109

Edwards, Cliff (c. 1895-1971), S18

Edwards, Ralph (1913--), T60, 20, 45

Eells, George (1922--), B110

Efron, Edith (1922--), B111

Eilers, Sally (1908-78), F16

Eisenhower, Dwight D. (1890-1969), S32, 11

Elder, Ann, T109

"Elephant Never Forgets, An," D43

Elias, Ellen (1950--), S45

Elinson, Jackie, T06

Elliott, Maurice, S21

"Embraceable You," T26

Emmons, Don, S36

Engebretson, Ollie, S31

Engel, Georgia, S45

Engel, Lehman (1910-82), B112

Engelbach, Dee (d. 1983), R16

Engle, Roy, F24

English, Joan, S14

Entertainment Hall of Fame (TV), T77, 46

Ephron, Henry (1911--), B116

Errett, Geoffrey, S23

Errol, Leon (1881-1951), F13, D03

Ethel Merman: A Musical Autobiography, D33, B545, 18

Ethel Merman & Mary Martin Duet from the Ford 50th Anniversary TV Show, D30, 18

Ethel Merman at Carnegie Hall D54

Ethel Merman Disco Album, The, D53, B43, B133, 21

Ethel Merman in Concert, S48, S49, S50, S52, S53, S54, S55, S56, S57, S58, S59, S60, S61, S62, S63, S64, S65, S66, S67, S68, S69, S70, S71, S72, S73, S74, S75, S76, S77, S78, S79, S80, S81, S82, S83, S84, S85, S86, S87, S88, S89, S90, S92, B157, B339, B472, B535, B591, 20

Ethel Merman in Concert at Carnegie Hall, S91, B32, B41, B319, B546, 20, 50

Ethel Merman/Lyda Roberti/Mae West (LP), D05

Ethel Merman on Broadway (TV), 17

Ethel Merman Show, The (radio), R14, B245, B311, B420, 16, 39

Ethel Merman Show, The (concert), S33, S37, S38, S39, S40, S41, S46, 15, 19, 40, 43

Ethel Merman Sings Cole Porter (LP), D06

Ethel Merman Sings the New Songs from Hello, Dolly! D47, 18

Ethel Merman: Songs She Has Made Famous, D25, 17

Ethel Merman: The World Is Your Balloon (LP), D28, 17

Ethel's Ridin' High (LP), D50, 21

Evans, David, S45

Evans, La Verne, S10

Evans, Neil, S17, S18, 21

Evening at the Pops (TV), T74

Evening with Ethel Merman, An (TV), T27

Everett, Jane, S26

Everton, Paul (1868-

Lupino, Ida (1918--),
F17
Lynch, Richard C.,
B282, B282
Lynn, Jim, S42
Lynn, Vera (1917--),
R21
Lynn, William (1889-
1952), S17, S29
Lysistrata, B228, B262
Lytell, Bert (c. 1885-
1954), R09

MacGowan, John
(c. 1896-1977), S10
MacGregor, Edgar (1879-
1957), S18, S27, S28
MacGregor, Kenneth
(d. 1968), R14
Mack, George E.
(c. 1866-1948), S21
MacLaine, Shirley
(1934--), T13
MacMurray, Fred (1908-
91), T78
MacRae, Gordon (1921-
86), T102
Macy, Carlton (1861-
1946), S10
Maggie Brown (TV), T32,
17, 43
Mainbocher (1891-1976),
S31
"Make It Another Old-
Fashioned, Please,"
T62, T79, D19, D20,
D33, D35, D42, 12
"Make the Man Love Me,"
D28
Mallee, Florence, S17,
S18
Malone, Elizabeth
(c. 1880-1955), S30
"Maloney, Hattie," S28,
T08, 12, 13
Malvern, Paul, F18
Malvin, Artie, T109
Manatt, Fred, S14
Mander, Raymond
(c. 1911-83), B283
"Mandy," D08
Maney, Richard (1891-
1968), B284

Mann, David (1916--),
S29
Manning, David
(1958--), S42
Manning, M., B285
Mantle, Burns (1873-
1948), B286, B287,
B288, B289, B290,
B291
Mantle, Russet, B292
"Marching Along with
Time," D16, 37
"Marching through Ber-
lin," F21, D21, 15
Mario, Paul, S29
Marion, George, Jr.
(1899-1968), F13
Marks, Marcia, B293
"Marrying for Love,"
R23, D26, D29
Marsac, Maurice, F25
Marshack, Les, T104
Marshall, Everett
(1901--), S14, 5
Marshall, Margaret
(d. 1951), B294
Marshall, Mort (1918-
79), S36
Martel, Remi, S29
Martha Dean Show, The
(radio), R26
Martin, Francis, F13,
F15, F16
Martin, George, S35
Martin, Gloria, S27
Martin, Mary (1913-90),
S32, S45, S51, R13,
T04, T81, T83, T99,
T111, T113, D30, D52,
B192, B295, 16, 20,
21, 40
Martin, Mary Joan, S17
Martin, Nan (1927--),
F26
Martin, Paul (c. 1900-
67), S29
Martin, Pete (c. 1901-
80), B308
Marx, Arthur (1893-
1964), B296
Marx, Groucho (1895-
1977), R23

"Parts I've Played,
The," D51
Pasetta, Marty, T109
Pastos, Spero (1940--),
B359
Patrick, Gail (1911-
80), F15
Patrick, Lee (1906-82),
F23
Patterson, Lee
(c. 1918-67), T39
Patterson, Lorna, F27
Pauncefort, George
(1870-1942), S18
Pavarotti, Luciano
(1935--), B360
Pavilion Royale, S08,
4, 32
Payn, Graham (1918--),
B361
Payne, Jacqueline, S45
Payne, Robert (1911-
83), B362
Peaker, E. J., T53
Pearson, Eppy, S28
Pegue, Paul, S17, S18
Peloquin, Noella, S31,
S35
Pendleton, Austin
(1940--), T84
Penman, Lea (1895-
1962), S30
Penn, Robert, S31
Pennington, Ron, B363
"People," D50
Perrin, Nat, F14, T09
Perry Como Show, The
(TV), T18, T22, T30,
B507
Person to Person (TV),
T12, 16, 41
Peters, Bernadette
(1948--), T82
Peters Sisters, F18
Petlack, Joan, S36
Phelps, Stowe, S31
Philadelphia Orchestra,
S90, 20, 48, 50
Philips, Mary (1901-
75), S21
Phillips, McCandlish,
B366, B367
Picture, Kay, S23

Pied Piper Award, T107,
B16, 22, 50
Pierce, Jack (1889-
1968), S30
Pierlot, Frank
(c. 1876-1955) F01
Pierre, Gloria, S14
Pincus, Irving
(d. 1984), S21
Pinza, Ezio (1892-
1957), R13
Pirie, Julia, S10, S17,
S18
Pitts, ZaSu (1898-
1963), F24
"Play a Simple Melody,"
D31
Pleasants, Henry
(1910--), B374
Poling, James, B375
Polk, Gordon (1924-60),
S35
Pollack, Lew (1895-
1946), F20
Pollock, Arthur
(1886--), B376
Polly Bergen Show, The
(TV), 149
Pond, Barbara, S27
Pons, Lily (1904-76),
12
Porter, A., B377
Porter, Cole (1891-
1964), F17, S21, S23,
S27, S28, S29, T07,
T08, T35, T77, T79,
D19, D34, D35, B110,
B185, B378, B463, 6,
7, 12, 13, 43, 46
Porter, Del, S10, S21
Porter, Richard, S36
Porter, Vivian, S10
Poston, Blanche, S17,
S18
Poston, Tom
(c. 1921--), T24
Power, Tyrone (1913-
58), F19
Powich, Christopher,
B233
Preminger, Erik Lee
(1944--), B415

"While Strolling through the Park One Day," D32
Whipple, Sidney (1888-1975), B571, B572
"Whispering," D50
White, George (1890-1968), S14, F02, 5
White, Jess (1918--), F24
Whiteman, Paul (1890-1967), B99
Whiting, Jack (1901-61), S18, S21
Whiting, Margaret (1924--), B574
Whiting, Richard (1891-1938), S17, S18, F15, F17
Whitney, Helene, S31, S35
Whitson, Beth Slater, F07
"Why Do They Call a Private a Private?" D22
"Why not String Along with Me?" D13
Wichita Symphony, S50, 47
Wickes, Mary (1916--), S26
Wiere Brothers, S33
Wieting, June, S29
Wilk, Max (1920--), B575
Williams, Mary Jane, S26
Williams, Rhys (1892-1969), F23
Wills, Lou, Jr. (1928--), S29
Wilson, Charles, F16
Wilson, Harry (d. 1978), S21
Wilson, John S. (1913--), B576
Wilson, Parker, S29, S30
Wilson, Roy, S35
Wilson, Teddy (1912-86), T04

Wiman, Dwight Deere (1895-1951), S26
Wiman, Nancy, S26
Winchell, Walter (1897-1972), B577
Winston, Pauline, S10
Winters, David (1939--), S36
Winters, Jonathan (1925--), F24, T13
Winters, Shelley (1922--), T94
"Wipe That Frown Right off Your Face," F08, D02
"With You on My Mind," D13
Wittop, Freddy (1921--), S45
Wodehouse, P. G. (1881-1975), S21, T07, B578
Wolfe, Anne, S23
Wood, Douglas (1880-1966), S17
Woodley, Mary, S30
Woolf, S. J. (1880-1948), B579
Woolsey, Robert (1889-1938), S10
"World Is Your Balloon, The," D28
World of Tomorrow, The (film), F27
"World, Take Me Back," 45, D47, 14
Worth, Billie (1917--), S31
Wyatt, Euphemia V. (1884-1978), B581, B582, B584, B585, B586, B587, B588
Wynn, Ed (1886-1966), F02, 7

Yarnell, Bruce (1935-73), S42, D46
York, Duke (d. 1952), F16
"You Appeal to Me," D12
"You Are the Music to the Words in My Heart," D12

About the Author

GEORGE B. BRYAN is a professor in the Department of Theatre at the University of Vermont and is Director of the Center for Research in Vermont. He is the author of *An Ibsen Companion: A Dictionary-Guide to the Life, Works, and Critical Reception of Henrik Ibsen* (Greenwood, 1984) and he compiled *Stage Lives: A Bibliography and Index to Theatrical Biographies in English* (Greenwood, 1985) and *Stage Deaths: A Biographical Guide to International Theatrical Obituaries, 1850 to 1990* (Greenwood, 1991). Bryan has published articles in *Shakespeare Quarterly*, *Theatre Studies*, *Theatre Arts*, and *Vermont History*.

Titles in Bio-Bibliographies in the Performing Arts

Milos Forman: A Bio-Bibliography
Thomas J. Slater

Kate Smith: A Bio-Bibliography
Michael R. Pitts

Patty Duke: A Bio-Bibliography
Stephen L. Eberly

Carole Lombard: A Bio-Bibliography
Robert D. Matzen

Eva Le Gallienne: A Bio-Bibliography
Robert A. Schanke

Julie Andrews: A Bio-Bibliography
Les Spindle

Richard Widmark: A Bio-Bibliography
Kim Holston

Orson Welles: A Bio-Bibliography
Bret Wood

Ann Sothern: A Bio-Bibliography
Margie Schultz

Alice Faye: A Bio-Bibliography
Barry Rivadue

Jennifer Jones: A Bio-Bibliography
Jeffrey L. Carrier

Cary Grant: A Bio-Bibliography
Beverley Bare Buehrer

Maureen O'Sullivan: A Bio-Bibliography
Connie J. Billips

Ava Gardner: A Bio-Bibliography
Karin J. Fowler

Jean Arthur: A Bio-Bibliography
Arthur Pierce and Douglas Swarthout

Donna Reed: A Bio-Bibliography
Brenda Scott Royce

Gordon MacRae: A Bio-Bibliography
Bruce R. Leiby

Mary Martin: A Bio-Bibliography
Barry Rivadue

Irene Dunne: A Bio-Bibliography
Margie Schultz

Anne Baxter: A Bio-Bibliography
Karin J. Fowler

Tallulah Bankhead: A Bio-Bibliography
Jeffrey L. Carrier

Jessica Tandy: A Bio-Bibliography
Milly S. Barranger

Janet Gaynor: A Bio-Bibliography
Connie Billips

James Stewart: A Bio-Bibliography
Gerard Molyneaux

Joseph Papp: A Bio-Bibliography
Barbara Lee Horn

Henry Fonda: A Bio-Bibliography
Kevin Sweeney

Edwin Booth: A Bio-Bibliography
L. Terry Oggel